South Africa
Weird and Wonderful

South Africa
Weird and
Wonderful

Rob Marsh

Tafelberg

To Mark, with love

Acknowlegements
This book could not have been written without the assistance of a number of people.
Although acknowledgements have been made in relevant footnotes, I would especially like
to express my gratitude to the following: Thalia Anderson, Inspector Francois Bakker,
Eric Bolsmann, LP (Bertus) Celliers, Dr Ronald Clarke, Steve de Agrela, Superintendent
Jan de Waal, Captain H Koekemoer, Johan le Roux, Martin Loots, Inspector Alwyn Olivier,
Captain GW. Prinsloo, Dean Riley-Hawkins, Mark Rose-Christie, Superintendent Sicro Schambriel,
Captain Tertius Stapelberg, Captain Joe Smith, Dr Himla Soodyall, Terence Stirling,
Johan Verhoef, the staff of the LP Neethling Building, the staff of the Sammy Marks Museum,
the staff of the Simonstown Museum, the Department of Defence Military History Photographic
Section, and Sian Tiley.

Photographic credits
Nigel Dennis: cover, pp 1, 2, 3
Die Beeld: pp. 58 (Jan Hamman), 81 (Marleen Noordergraaf), 84 (Leon Botha), 135 (Robbie Schneider);
Die Burger: pp. 36, 49, 60 (Johann van Tonder), 62 (Robertson), 68; Mark de Lange (illustrations): pp. 7
(map), 12, 21 (map), 22, 26, 30 (map), 47, 56, 57 (map), 70, 77, 82, 87, 95, 110, 117 (map), 127, 131
(map); Department of Defence Military History Photographic Section: p. 40; Amanda Esterhuysen/
University of the Witwatersrand: pp. 108, 109, 111; Jonathan Ball Publishers: pp. 54, 55 (*Jock of the
Bushveld* by Percy Fitzpatrick, illustrations by Edmond Caldwell, published by Ad Donker Publishers,
1907); Johan le Roux: pp. 138 (illustration), 139, 140, 141; Beefy Mance: p. 64; Marius Loots: pp. 12,
14, 16, 17, 18; Rob Marsh: pp. 53, 67, 72, 73, 76, 96, 97, 104, 122, 124; Namdeb Diamond
Corporation: p. 106; Simonstown Museum: pp. 51, 52, 53; South African Library: pp. 20 (*Travels and
Adventures in Eastern Africa* by Nathaniel Isaacs, 1836), 24, 29, 33, 73, 79, 113, 114 (*Narrative of a
Voyage of Observation* by James Alexander, 1837), 119, 120; University of Pretoria – Centre for
Indigenous Knowledge Mapungubwe Collection: pp. 6, 7, 8, 9, 10, 11.

First Published in 2003 by

Tafelberg Publishers
28 Wale Street, Cape Town 8000
Registration nr.: 51/02378/06

10 9 8 7 6 5 4 3 2 1

Publisher Anita Pyke
Editor Sean Fraser
Production Andrew de Kock
Cover design Michiel Botha
Design and typesetting Alinea Studio, Cape Town
Reproduction by Unifoto (Pty) Ltd, Cape Town
Printed and bound by Tien Wah Press (Pte) Ltd, Singapore

ISBN 0 624040682

Contents

Wrecks and Ruins

Disasters happen. Accidents occur. Motorcars collide, aeroplanes fall out of the sky, ships sink and nations decline and fall. In the end, all we are left with to mark their passing are the wrecks and ruins they leave behind. On the following pages, we will examine some of the more noteworthy occurrences that have, over the years, profoundly affected the lives of ordinary South Africans, and, in some instances, even changed the course of history.[1]

Mapungubwe: South Africa's first city

To the Sesotho people, Mapungubwe translates as 'Hill of the Jackal'. In TshiVenda, the word means 'Place of Stone'. The ancient citadel, which lies about 100 kilometres west of Messina in Limpopo Province, has been described as one of the most precious archaeological sites in South Africa, and yet for almost 60 years – from the late 1930s to the middle of the 1990s – the South African government kept Mapungubwe out of the public consciousness. For this reason very few people have heard of Mapungubwe. Fewer still understand its significance to South Africa's national heritage.

Why is Mapungubwe special?

'It is not common in the archaeological world that you can actually pinpoint and say: "This is the place where society transformed from one quite different kind of organisation to another". That's one of the things that makes this place absolutely unique.' These were the words of Professor Tom Huffman in 2001.

Mapungubwe, at the height of its power for only 60 to 80 years during the 13th century, was South Africa's first Egoli – a place where gold was smelted 600 years before Johannesburg was established. Indeed, the crafting of gold was to become the trademark of Mapungubwe. It was also the centre of an important trading area, and probably the first location in southern Africa where cotton was grown and woven into cloth. More significantly still, Mapungubwe was a place where southern African society was 'transformed from one kind of organisation to another', where for the first time in southern Africa a king ruled over his subjects and, in turn, was venerated by them.

Top right Decorated, punched, half-moon-shaped gold-foil plates were found in the royal burial site in 1934. They measure about three centimetres across and their use is unknown.
Below The sandstone hill of Mapungubwe is approximately 30 metres high and 300 metres long.

A time of change…

Mapungubwe is located at the confluence of the Shashe and Limpopo rivers in the Limpopo-Shashe basin, an area of high temperatures and relatively low rainfall where droughts are not uncommon. People first settled in the Limpopo valley in about 200 AD and by 900 AD major permanent settlements had been established, with domesticated animals providing up to 90 per cent of the meat consumed by the local populace.

As traders and merchants from the east coast travelled further and further inland, the area grew in importance, and by around the 8th or 9th century AD the region's first settlement had been established at Schroda, on a rocky plateau overlooking the Limpopo River. Schroda, which takes its name from the farming settlement on which the site is located, had a population of between 500 and 700 and is thought to have been the largest settlement in southern Africa at the time.

In around 1000 AD, Schroda was, however, invaded and its inhabitants were forced to flee westwards, effectively cutting them off from the east-coast trade and, as Schroda declined, another settlement called K2 (named by an early excavator who said the area reminded him of the settlement *koms* of North Africa) rose to prominence nearby. Up until this time, cattle had been the traditional form of wealth, but at K2 they moved to the periphery of the economy and glass beads and gold replaced livestock as the most important form of stored wealth. And, because the keeping and trading of these commodities was effectively restricted to a relatively small group, an unequal distribution of wealth occurred and class distinctions emerged. Eventually, the king and the royal family were to be completely separated from the people, the dichotomy between the rulers and the ruled being further exacerbated when overcrowding in the small valley in which K2 was situated encouraged the ruling elite to relocate to Mapungubwe.

This move occurred sometime around 1075 AD. The first houses were built beneath the hill the new settlers called Mapungubwe, but in time these were extended onto the summit and then, for the next 60–80 years, Mapungubwe became the richest and most powerful settlement in the region.

Above Human clay figurine may well have been used in initiation rituals. Hundreds of figurines, ranging in size from four centimetres to 19 centimetres, were found at Mapungubwe.
Left The ancient settlement of Mapungubwe was situated just south of the Limpopo River.

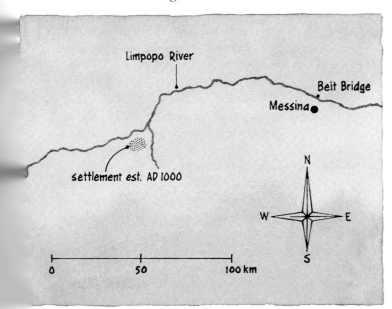

Limpopo River

Beit Bridge

Messina

settlement est. AD 1000

N
W — E
S

0   50   100 km

'To climb the mountain you must go zigzag'

During the period when the Mapungubwe settlement was at the height of its power and influence, it had an estimated population of 3000–5000 and covered an empire of more than 30 000 square kilometres. The vast majority of its people lived on the plain surrounding the hill, with only the ruling elite living on the mount itself. The king and his retinue stayed on the summit, where they were isolated and protected, while members of the royal family

Did you know?

The ruins of the ancient city of Mapungubwe in Limpopo Province comprise one of the most important prehistoric sites in South Africa and are thought to have been established about 1000 years ago.

occupied the terraces below. Interestingly, a reminder of this period is a Venda saying that still survives today: 'To climb the mountain you must go zigzag', which means that to approach the king one must use an intermediary.

By physically separating themselves from the 'common' people – there is only a narrow twisting path to the summit – the king and his supporters increased both their status and their power. Significantly, this physical separation would have also indirectly reinforced the ritualisation of leadership, which was a new development in the culture of the region. It is also likely that the king alone was authorised to communicate with the ancestors: a position of supreme power, since it was the ancestors who communicated with god!

Trade with the coast

Islamic seafarers from India and the Middle East probably began to explore the east coast of Africa about 2000 years ago, with the seasonal monsoon winds carrying them across the Indian Ocean. These traders brought with them cargoes of beads, cloth and glazed pottery, which they exchanged on the African coast for gold, ivory and animal skins. Unfortunately, the earliest accounts of this trade are somewhat unreliable having, in the main, been passed down by word of mouth. In the *Periplus of the Erythraean Sea*, a guide to the ports of Arabia, India and East Africa written in about 100 AD, for example, reference is made to the port of Rhapta on the coast of Africa, where 'much ivory and tortoiseshell'[2] was to be obtained. Unfortunately, the precise location of Rhapta remains a mystery, although some historians believe it to have been situated somewhere on the coast of modern Tanzania.

What is known is that by 900 AD, Islamic seafarers had sailed as far south as Sofala in present-day Mozambique, and trade with the interior was firmly established. By 1200 AD, however, the coastal belt was almost exhausted for trading purposes and merchants began to look further inland. It was this development that led to the growth of Schroda, K2 and, finally, Mapungubwe.

Below Among the selection of clay artefacts found at the site was a doughnut-shaped object (bottom right) originally used as a spindle whorl for spinning cotton.

The actual mechanics of the trade are less well known. Certainly, a number of goods would have been exchanged at markets in major towns in the region, but the Arab geographer Abdullah al-Idrisi also claimed that Muslim traders knew of a number of landing and collection points along the coast. These would quite probably have included the estuary of the Zambezi River, and possibly also the Limpopo.

Ivory and animal skins

Ivory and animal skins were probably the first exports from the Limpopo valley and these were much in demand in Muslim countries. Ivory, in particular, was probably the centre of the thriving economy at Mapungubwe and, in all likelihood, was the region's main export. Ivory bracelets have been found at K2 and a large number of bone tools, especially needles, appear to have been produced for export.

There is also an interesting account by Al-Mas'udi, an Arab trader who visited the east coast in the 10th century [AD], of an elephant hunt, which may have been typical of those carried out in the Limpopo valley.

'There are many wild elephants but no tame ones. The Zanj [people of "the land of Zanj" – Africa] do not use them for war or anything else, but only hunt and kill them. When they want to catch them they throw down the leaves, bark and branches of a certain tree which grows in the country: then they wait in ambush until the elephants come down to drink. The water burns them and makes them drunk. They fall down and cannot get up: their limbs will not articulate. The Zanj rush upon them armed with very long spears, and kill them for their ivory. It is from this country that come tusks weighing fifty pounds and more.'[3]

The decline and fall of Mapungubwe

After less than a century as the most powerful city-state in the region, Mapungubwe's power and status began to wane. The reason for this is not clear, but was probably the result of a combination of factors, most significantly a change in climate – leading to cooler temperatures and less rainfall, which made growing crops more difficult – and a shift in power northwards and across the Limpopo to the settlement we now call Great Zimbabwe.

Whatever the reason, by 1300 AD Mapungubwe had virtually ceased to exist and would remain all but forgotten for over 600 years.

The 20th century: Secrecy and denial

Legends that a king's ransom in gold lay hidden somewhere in or around Mapungubwe persisted well into the 20th century and these stories, stimulated no doubt by talk of King Solomon's mines and the discovery of the gold fields in and around Johannesburg, brought a stream of European prospectors into the area, though with markedly little success.

In 1932, however, this was all to change. In that year, a teacher, Jerry van Graan, and his friends decided to investigate Mapungubwe for themselves. Ignoring warnings from the local Venda that certain death would befall anyone who ventured onto the hill, they climbed to the summit, and it was here, at the site of what would later be recognised as the royal burial ground, that they discovered golden treasures weighing over two kilograms. These artefacts they divided upon among themselves.

Fortunately, the son of one of the three men was a University of Pretoria student and sent a letter describing their find, and including a small fragment of gold he had unearthed, to his professor, Leo Fouché. Fouché immediately realised the 'great significance' of the find and, shortly afterward, Professor Lowe of the University of the Witswatersrand visited the area, also labelling Mapungubwe a place of 'great importance'.

The diggings begin

The first excavations at Mapungubwe were carried out between 1933 and 1935, when the government of the Union of South Africa acquired the farm on which Mapungubwe stood and appointed the University of Pretoria as its nominated authority to carry out a formal investigation.

The first graves were discovered soon after the diggings had begun and in 1936 the archaeology committee at the University of Pretoria put a golden rhinoceros found at the site on display at the Transvaal Museum. A year later, Fouché

Above All ceramicware found at Mapungubwe was hand moulded by the women of the settlement.

King Solomon and Queen Sheba

According to the Old Testament, King Solomon was the third king of Israel and the son of David by Bathsheba. He was famed for his wisdom and his alliances with Egypt and Phoenicia brought a prolonged period of peace to the region.

The Queen of Sheba was thought by the Romans to have ruled over the Sabeaens in the ancient kingdom of Sha'abijah (now south Yemen), an area once renowned for its gold and spices. According to 1 Kings X, in the Bible, the Queen of Sheba visited King Solomon and until 1975 the Ethiopian royal house traced its descent to their union.

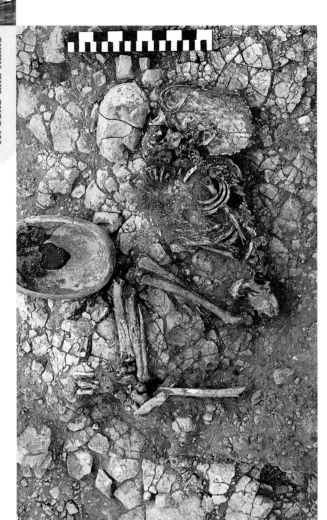

Above Bodies were usually buried with a selection of ceramicware, imported trade glass beads and shells. Only royalty was buried with gold.

published a report on the site, which was titled: 'Mapungubwe – An ancient Bantu civilisation on the Limpopo.' In this report, Fouché argued that Mapungubwe had clear links to Tswana and Sotho cultures and was obviously of African origin. He also said that the site was less than 200 years old and the settlement founded there had been established after that at Great Zimbabwe. Both these theories were, however, later proved false and only in 1959 did radiocarbon tests prove the age of a kingdom flourishing 1000 years ago.

The Mapungubwe Collection, including the golden rhinoceros, had never been permanently displayed for public viewing and had been locked away in a vault at Pretoria University, and was to remain unexhibited for 60 years until June 2000, when the University of Pretoria launched the Mapungubwe Museum.

The conspiracy of silence

It was obvious that Mapungubwe was a site of considerable black achievement but the powers-that-were refused to accept this fact. Black people in the 13th century were simply incapable of such advanced work, many argued. The conclusion, therefore, was obvious: Mapungubwe was the result of outside – that is, Egyptian or possibly European – influence.

In 1935, Captain Guy Gardner was appointed to excavate the site, a task he carried out until 1940. Unfortunately, Gardner's methods were extremely destructive. Trenches were dug but two-thirds of the material removed from the ground was unceremoniously dumped over the side of the hill without sifting. Numerous problems, however, hampered his research from 1933 to 1940. During this time, there were virtually no professional archaeologists working in South Africa; many an excavation season was also hampered by outbreaks of malaria, and concerns for the outbreak of war. Gardner also held onto a number of preconceptions: the site, Gardner argued, was neither ancient, nor Bantu. K2 was instead the product of 'Hottentot' culture, and most likely the work of the 'Hottentot' who had migrated to the region from elsewhere. In Gardner's opinion, an Nguni community absorbed some of the K2 Hottentots, where they eventually established an empire at Mapungubwe.

Despite scientific evidence to the contrary, Gardner encouraged people to identify Mapungubwe with Great Zimbabwe and, by association, with ancient Egypt and Europe. This theory – that Great Zimbabwe had been constructed by Sabaeans and Phoenicians and after a transitional phase had been occupied by a 'bastard race' – had been put forward over 30 years earlier by R N Hall, a journalist, and W G Neal, a prospector, who had carried out excavations at Great Zimbabwe.

This, of course, was all part of a much larger race debate. Gardener, like so many of his contemporaries, also argued that Bantus were not living in the area at the time and, to lend credence to this theory, he created new names for these 'Hottentot migrants', whom he maintained had moved into the area 600–700 years before. He referred to them as Proto-Hottentot and Bush-Boskopoid peoples. Significantly, perhaps, Gardner's report, which was concluded in 1940, was only published 23 years later, in 1963, after the outbreak of World War II and was perhaps delayed due to Gardner's fight with cancer.

Mapungubwe under apartheid

By the late 1960s the apartheid government was defending itself against the rise of both nationalism and communism and Mapungubwe was part of a state-owned farm named Greefswald, which was appropriated by the South African Defence Force in 1968. The Defence Force, however, granted permission for archaeological research on the condition that all responsibility remained with the University of Pretoria, and the University undertook to erect fences around the site, which was out of bounds to military personnel. Needless to say, with the site now under the control of the South African army, access to the area was severely restricted.

In 1969, the University of Pretoria established an archaeology department, and the excavations at Mapungubwe continued for the following 25 years, though under something of a veil of secrecy. Unfortunately, many of the academic publications were not published under apartheid rule, and the media claimed that this was a systematic attempt to deny black South Africans their heritage. Under apartheid, school textbooks started the story of South Africa's history in 1652, when Jan van Riebeeck arrived in what is today Cape Town to establish a trading post. They paid scant attention to the history of native inhabitants of southern Africa. Mapungubwe was eventually, however, declared a National Heritage Site in 1984, and the artefacts and bones unearthed there have now been systematically recorded and catalogued, and are on display at the University of Pretoria.

The search for gold

There are at least half a dozen ancient gold mines north and south of the Limpopo, but their outputs were, in all probability, extremely limited. An Indonesian seafaring expedition that arrived at the coast near Sofala in the 10th century, for example, came to acquire ivory, tortoiseshell, leopard skins and ambergris, among other things, but there is no evidence indicating that it encountered gold, possibly suggesting that this commodity was not necessarily associated with the region.

Nevertheless, by the beginning of the 13th century, gold had become a sought-after commodity. Archaeological evidence suggests that the people of Mapungubwe were already skilled in smelting hard metals, so it would have been easy to smelt gold – but gold was not easy to come by. In all likelihood, most of the gold produced in the area would have been panned from alluvial deposits or mined from gold-bearing quartz reefs located in the region. Extracting the gold ore, however, would have been difficult and labour intensive because the process involved heating the quartz, then crushing and separating the ore, which was then broken out with iron pikes and lifted to the surface in baskets. For this reason, gold mining is likely to have been a seasonal rather than a full-time occupation and would only have been undertaken when labour was not required in the fields.

Bottom Among the gold treasures from the royal burial site were three rhinos, only one of which was restored. Because of the delicate and specialised work required, the rhino was restored by experts at the British Museum.

The treasures of Mapungubwe

A number of exquisitely worked gold objects, most notably the golden bowl, the golden rhino and the golden 'sceptre' were discovered in graves on the summit of Mapungubwe. The objects are made up of gold sheeting laid over wood and held in place with solid gold nails. Today, these have been declared national treasures.

While gold artefacts are probably the most celebrated of Mapungubwe's treasures, a number of other significants finds were made at the ancient site, not the least of which were the age-old spindle whorls – clay discs with a hole in the middle – which were twirled and used to pull cotton from the cotton boll. In fact, the Limpopo valley is the oldest site in the country at which spindle whorls have been found, suggesting that Mapungubwe and its surrounds was the first place in southern Africa where cotton was cultivated.

Grave sites also proved an extraordinarily rich archaeological find, despite the fact that the last king was buried at Mapungubwe some 800 years ago. At the so-called royal cemetery on the hilltop, 23 bodies have been discovered and in three of these graves gold objects such as the gold rhino, the gold bowl, the gold sceptre and various items of jewellery accompanied the bodies.

It is also clear from diggings that glass beads were valuable commodities, which were only obtainable through trade with the east coast. At Schroda, beads were used as a new currency and to barter and trade. More glass beads have been found at Schroda than any other archaeological site in southern Africa. Later, however, the people of K2 began to manufacture their own beads.

Thulamela: The place of birth

Thulamela is a Karanga word that means 'hill with no vegetation' or 'the place of giving birth' and, of these, the latter is generally favoured as the modern translation, especially given the fact that, in the ancient tradition of the Shona/Karanga people, metalworking is seen as a birth process.

Located on the summit of a rocky hilltop near Pafuri, over-looking what is now the common border with Mozambique and Zimbabwe, at the northern end of the Kruger National Park, the original settlement at Thulamela was inhabited from the 13th to the 16th centuries. Since the early 1990s, Thulamela has been carefully excavated, and in part reconstructed, primarily by South African National Parks (SANP) and – in a first for South African archaeology – representatives of the local community, who may be descendants of Thulamela's people. So far, the well-preserved skeletons of two individuals – a male and a female – have been discovered here, along with about 150 grams of gold, including a number of beautiful gold wire bangles and gold beads.

Top right Beads and other hand-crafted artefacts were common forms of currency in Thulamela. *Below* The original settlement at Thulamela proved to be an important trading centre between communities on the east coast and West Africa.

The site was clearly an important trading centre, but Thulamela also has clear cultural links to both the earlier settlement at Mapungubwe, and to Great Zimbabwe, with which it co-existed. It has thus provided scientists with a wealth of detail about the indigenous inhabitants who occupied this part of the African continent approximately 500–700 years ago, but what is equally significant is the fact that the people of ancient Thulamela had a highly organised society and were exchanging goods with both West Africa and countries as far away as India and China.

Ancient settlements

For thousands of years, Thulamela was a wild and lonely place visited only by animals, and a settlement was first established at the site about 800 years ago in about 1200 AD. In this earliest phase, the people of Thulamela did not build walls and there is no evidence that they engaged in trade. In fact, the first stone terraces were probably built only 200 years later, in around 1400 AD, at the same time that Great Zimbabwe was flourishing. It was also during this period that the people of Thulamela began to develop trade links with the outside world, including India, from where glass beads were imported.

As was the case at Mapungubwe, it seems that the chief and his family eventually took up residence on the summit of the hill, surrounded by some 1500 of his immediate subjects, who lived on and around the slopes below.

Between 1400–1600 AD, Thulamela was at the height of its power and had become a centre for trade in the area, with evidence indicating that inhabitants were skilled goldsmiths. Artefacts found at the site include beautifully wrought gold bracelets and beads, harpoons to hunt hippo, royal gongs from West Africa, pieces of porcelain from the Ming Dynasty in China and beads from India.

Over the last decade, Thulamela has been described as a 'mountain fastness' and the heart of a 'divine kingdom', but the reality is somewhat more prosaic. It would be more accurate to say that Thulamela was a fairly typical hilltop site, and representative of a number of similar sites in the region.

Rediscovery and excavation

Thulamela was abandoned – possibly following an attack by invaders from a neighbouring region – sometime during the 17th century and the site lay abandoned for over 200 years, but in 1983, Dr Pienaar, Park Warden at the Kruger National Park, began conducting an audit of all historical and prehistoric sites within the park. To this end, rangers and other park staff were asked to assist with the identification and plotting of any places of special significance, and it was during this exercise that Thulamela was first identified as a site of noteworthy interest.

In 1991, interest in the area was rekindled and a preliminary investigation into the site was conducted. Thulamela was thus declared a cultural site of national significance and a project committee was set up.

While the primary participants in the Thulamela project were South African National Parks, with Sidney Miller as chief archaeologist, and Gold Fields South Africa, which funded the entire exercise, a number of other parties were also consulted, including the local community (which provided important oral evidence), the University of Cape Town (which did metallurgic analysis on the artefacts unearthed) and the University of Pretoria (which was brought in to excavate the graves). Apart from anything else, the Thulamela project provided a good example of how the top experts in various fields can be used to ensure work of the highest quality.

Did you know?

For more than 200 years, Thulamela was one of the most important trading centres in southern Africa and is now a cultural site of national importance.

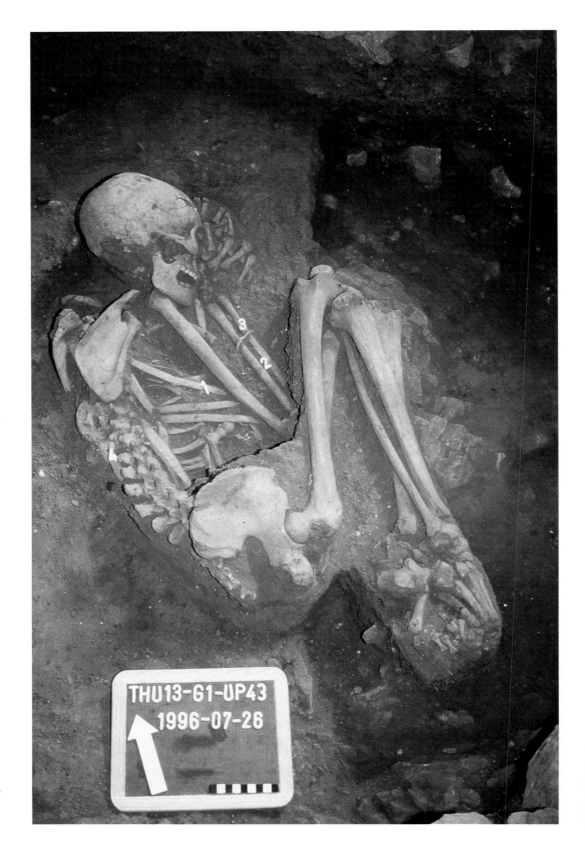

Right Workers on the site from which she was unearthed named this female 'Losha', after the name for the position of respect – palms pressed together and placed next to the left temple – in which she was placed.

The excavations that subsequently took place were conducted in two stages. The first stage was an 'exploratory' excavation, which was followed in 1993 by a second 'official' excavation, carried out under the direction of Sidney Miller. Small gold beads, golden wire and potsherd with traces of molten gold were discovered and then, in July 1996, the first major find took place. This was the discovery of an articulated skeleton – later called 'Losha' – in the Queen's Enclosure, usually referred to as Enclosure 5. The body, which had been placed horizontally in the ground in a foetal position, was accompanied by 291 gold beads and a triple-woven golden bracelet.

Losha

Traditionally, Venda women pay respect to men by bowing slightly with their palms pressed together and their hands placed next to the left temple. This respectful posture is called the losha and was mirrored in the position that the skeleton had been placed at burial. For this reason, some of the workers at the site began referring to the remains as 'Losha', and the name stuck.

Very little is, however, known about Losha other than that she was female, between 45 and 60 years of age and about 1,73 metres tall. She had good, strong teeth and appeared to have been in good health, with no sign of osteoporosis. Who 'Losha' was or what duties she performed remains a mystery. However, given the Vendas' settlement patterns, the place where her body was found could loosely be described as a 'wives' or 'female' area. It was for this reason that the area became known as the Queen's Enclosure.

A second grave is discovered

Two months after the discovery of 'Losha', a male skeleton, which was later named 'Ingwe' (leopard), was uncovered in the 'Royal Enclosure'. This second body was also accompanied by various items of jewellery, but – unlike Losha's skeleton – had completely decomposed and a number of the bones, which were separated at the joints, were not located in the correct anatomical positions: they appeared to have been carefully placed in the ground, using the skull as a kind of centrepiece.

This unusual arrangement could be explained by reference to an ancient Venda custom in which the body of an important person would be wrapped in cowhide and left in his or her hut until both the body and the hut fell apart. Eventually – probably about nine months after death – the skeleton would then be reburied, sometimes in situ. Significantly, both the so-called Royal Enclosure where Ingwe was discovered and the Queen's Enclosure where Losha was unearthed are situated in the most isolated parts of the citadel and these areas are now thought to have been the living quarters of a chief and his senior wife. The final interpretation by Miller is that this area originally functioned as the *pfamo* or private quarters for the chief and his immediate family. This would have been the area where the chief slept and where the most important tribal relics and religious ornaments were kept.

The sacred king

The layout and construction of Thulamela provides important insights into the social organisation of the people who lived there. The so-called Royal Enclosure, for example, was located at the northern end of the site, on the edge of steep cliffs, suggesting that the chief remained in seclusion and may rarely, if ever, have been seen in public. In all likelihood, visitors would have approached the chief by climbing a zigzag path to the hill summit and entered the citadel at the southern end, all the time under the watchful eye of the chief's bodyguard, possibly led by the chief's brother. Having crossed the main enclosure, visitors would then have had to enter the chief's audience chamber on their stomachs as a mark of respect. And, after the audience was over, they would have retreated in the same way, never once turning their backs.

Interestingly, though, there appears to have been a dividing wall of some sort in the chief's audience chamber and there is a possibility that visitors would never have actually seen the chief, but would have communicated with him through this wall, or possibly through an intermediary.

While it would make for a more romantic telling, it is, however, important to remember that it is unlikely that either Losha or Ingwe were of royal blood, and would not have enjoyed the reverence given to a king or queen. Their names – taken to mean 'king' and 'queen' – were merely codes that were romanticised by the media, and Losha and Ingwe, in fact, lived some 150 years apart.

Given the relatively small size of Thulamela, it is unlikely that Ingwe would have been a 'king', though he may have held the status of a chief. Similarly, Losha was probably no more than a very senior (royal) wife. In the case of both Ingwe and Losha, neither their true names nor the causes of their deaths have been established.

Thulamela today...

According to South African legislation, only a certain portion of any archaeological site may be excavated in a given period of time. Since archaeology is considered a 'destructive' science, this practice ensures that some deposits are left for later investigations with (quite possibly) better techniques and different questions, etc.

The stone walls at Thulamela have been painstakingly rebuilt, using original materials, but all further work at the site has ceased. There are currently no plans to carry out further excavations in the near future.

Trade with the East

By the time that Thulamela had risen to prominence, trade links with the Middle and Far East were already firmly established – a fact confirmed by one of the most remarkable travellers of all time, Ibn Battuta. Ibn Battuta was born in Tangier in 1304 and, after being educated as a lawyer, embarked on a pilgrimage to Mecca, the Muslim holy city. This long journey was to initiate a lifetime of travel during which he criss-crossed the Muslim world, visiting in the process some of its most remote outposts.

At the age of 21, Ibn Battuta journeyed down the Nile from Alexandria to Cairo and then, in due course, to Damascus and Basra. Later, he embarked on his first long sea voyage – to Somalia and then along the East African coast as far south as Tanzania. In fact, it was during this voyage that remarked upon the difficult relations that existed between the Muslim traders in the area and the 'pagan' Africans whom they enslaved.

Below A fine selection of meticulously crafted gold jewellery was unearthed at the Thulamela archaeological site.

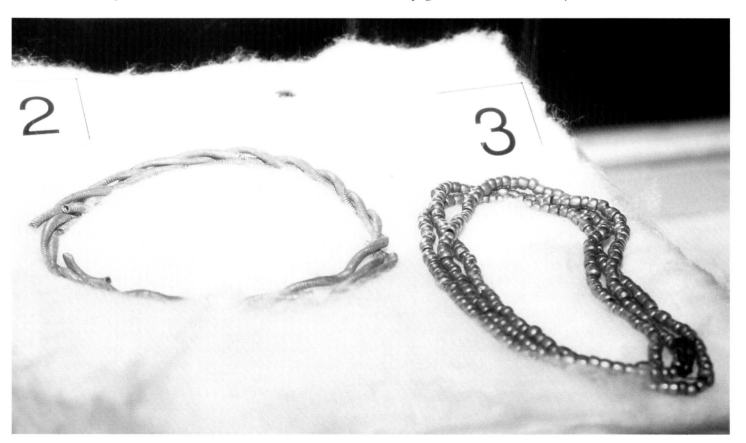

He later crossed the Arabian Sea and travelled to Oman and the port of Hormuz. Between 1349 and 1354 Ibn Battuta travelled to India and, later on, to China, though apparently without much enthusiasm:

'China was beautiful, but it did not please me. On the contrary, I was greatly troubled, thinking about the way paganism dominated this country. Whenever I went out of my lodgings, I saw many blameworthy things. That disturbed me so much that I stayed indoors most of the time and only went out when necessary.'[4]

It would be wrong, however, to assume that trade was entirely monopolised by Islamic travellers. Chinese merchants – among others – placed much greater emphasis on boat building and huge sea-going junks began to roam the South China Sea and the Indian and Pacific Oceans, and travelling to the African coast on a fairly regular basis. In fact, it was during the early 15th century that one of China's greatest sailors, Admiral Zheng Ho, visited Borneo, Java, Sumatra, India and the Middle East. Between 1405 and 1433 Zheng Ho led no less than seven fleets, some consisting of over 60 ships, across the China Sea and Indian Ocean. It was from one of these journeys that he returned to China with a giraffe, which he presented to the Emperor.

Above Although little remains of the original site today, the Thulamela citadel proved a treasure house of extraordinary archaeological finds that revealed a long-forgotten people and their remarkable culture.

King Solomon's gold

According to the Bible (1 Kings 5:3), King Solomon (*circa* 974–934 BC), the third king of Israel and the son of King David by Bathsheba, tasked himself with the building of a fine temple, which was to be dedicated to '...the worship of the Lord my God'. To this end, he sent men to 'Lebanon' to cut down cedars, acquired stone from nearby quarries and then, using masons from the cities of Tyre and Byblos, began construction. Seven years later, the temple was complete. Solomon had used gold to overlay the walls, the rafters and the thresholds, and even the floor was allegedly covered with gold. According to 1 Kings 6:21–22, 'gold chains were placed across the entrance of the inner room, which was also covered with gold. The whole interior of the temple was covered with gold, as well as the altar in the Holy of Holies'.

Some 300 years later, the temple was looted and destroyed by the invading Babylonians. A second temple was eventually built on the same site by King Herod the Great, but this building was also later destroyed. The question, however remains that if the Bible's description of the temple is accurate, then where did Solomon obtain his gold? According to 2 Chronicles (3:3–13), it was imported from 'the land of Parvaim'. Unfortunately, the location of 'the land of Parvaim' has never been established. Some scholars suggest that this was merely a reference to the 'Oriental regions' of Arabia. Others suggest it may be linked to the fabled port of Ophir.

Fabled Ophir

Ophir was a seaport or region from which, allegedly, Solomon's ships brought not only fine gold in great quantity, but also sandalwood, precious stones, ivory, apes and peacocks, but the precise location of of the port remains unknown – although many areas of the Arabian peninsula and India have been proposed. The present tendency is to identify it with Yemen in southeast Arabia and possibly with the neighbouring African coast, and the fact that many Egyptian pharaohs sent naval expeditions to Punt (Somalia) for monkeys, ivory, frankincense and slaves, gives credence to the suggestion that Ophir was indeed an East African site.

The myth persists

Interestingly, the legend of King Solomon's riches and his links with the continent of Africa were resurrected yet again during the 19th century with the publication of the widely aclaimed novel, *King Solomon's Mines*, written by Rider Haggard in 1885. In this book, three European heroes – Sir Henry Curtis, Captain John Good, R N and the narrator, Allan Quartermain – set off into the interior of the Dark Continent to find Curtis's missing brother George who has gone to look, unsuccessfully, it will later turn out, for lost treasure of King Solomon's mines.

Top right Gold artefacts and jewellery, such as these golden necklaces and beads found at Thulamela, help to fuel speculation about lost African treasures even today.

Did you know?

According to the Bible, the Queen of Sheba visited King Solomon and until 1975 the Ethiopian royal house traced its descent to their union.

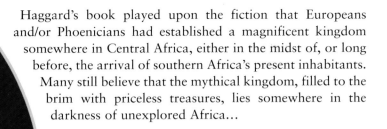

Haggard's book played upon the fiction that Europeans and/or Phoenicians had established a magnificent kingdom somewhere in Central Africa, either in the midst of, or long before, the arrival of southern Africa's present inhabitants. Many still believe that the mythical kingdom, filled to the brim with priceless treasures, lies somewhere in the darkness of unexplored Africa...

The legend of Prester John

The story of Prester John, supposedly a fabulously wealthy descendant of the Magi, who lived in the Orient, first arose during the period of the Crusades (late 11th–13th centuries) and, in essence, tells that, once upon a time in a very remote land, there was a king who was not only a great king but a Christian priest as well. The name of the king was Prester John and he ruled a vast empire, rich in silver and gold.

The story begins around 1145 when Hugh, Bishop of Gebal (modern Jabala in Lebanon), visited Pope Eugenius at the Papal court in Viterbo, Italy, to ask for help against the Turkish, who were threatening to overrun the Holy Land. In an account of this meeting written by Bishop Otto of Freisling, Germany, reference was made to a 'priest and king' who had visited the Christ child, defeated the Muslim kings of Persia in battle and intended to march on Jeruselem, but was being held up at the banks of the river Tigris.

In a later development in 1165, a forged letter – allegedly from Prester John – was delivered to Emperor Manuel Comnenus of Byzantium, who forwarded it to Emperor Frederic Babarous of the Holy Roman Empire.

The forger was clever in that he (or she) repeated many of the same stories detailed in Bishop Otto's report and played upon the same hopes and fears of Christians vis-à-vis the infidel Turks. He (or she) also underscored the riches of Prester John's kingdom by declaring, 'for gold, silver, precious stones, animals of every kind and the number of our people, we believe there is not our equal under heaven'.

In the mid-13th century, when the Crusades had ended and Asia had again become accessible to Europe, a search was conducted to find Prester John, primarily with a view to re-establishing ties with China through his intervention. Not surprisingly, however, Prester John was never found, but the legends and rumours concerning his existence, continued to flourish throughout the Middle Ages. In fact, in the 14th century, when all searches in Asia had turned up empty, it was assumed that Prester John was being sought for in the wrong region and attention then shifted to Africa, Ethiopia in particular. Such was the belief in the legend, the Portugese allegedly looked for Prester John all over Africa in the 15th century.

Discovering the dates

With all the talk of ancient treasures and historically significant artefacts unearthed from some of Africa's greatest heritage sites, how do we know that these pieces do in fact form part of our cultural legacy? One way of determining the age of organic archaeological finds such as bone and wooden items is by radiocarbon dating, a process that was discovered by Willard Libby in 1947. Plants assimilate from the atmosphere carbon dioxide, a small proportion of which is the isotope Carbon-14. This isotope is then incorporated into the plant tissue. Animals, for their part, absorb Carbon-14 when they consume plant tissue. On death, the plant ceases to take up Carbon-14 and that already absorbed begins to decay at a known rate. After 120 000 years, the amount of Carbon-14 remaining in a sample is virtually immeasurable. Although there is some scientific debate surrounding the issue, the accuracy of radiocarbon dating is thought to be reasonably reliable – to an accuracy of about 80 years – for artefacts dating to between 5000 and 60 000 years ago.

The legend of Sudwala Caves

Located between Middelburg and Nelspruit in Mpumalanga in a range of mountains known as the Mankelekele, which means 'crag on crag', the Sudwala Caves overlook the Houtbosloop, a tributary of the Crocodile River and are a stone's throw from the N4 highway. They were formed by a process of water and chemical erosion about 200 million years ago and still go through 'dry' and 'wet' periods, depending on the weather.

There is also evidence that the ancient Sudwala Caves have been occupied by human inhabitants for as long as 1,8 million years, excavations at the site have revealing a fine collection of stone tools – probably crafted by *Australopithecus habilis* – which are now on display at the cave entrance.

Background to conflict

The original inhabitants of modern Swaziland were the San, but by the 16th century these people had largely moved away and been replaced by the Sotho and, after about 200 years, the Sotho were in turn replaced as the dominant group in the region by the Swazi. This latter change took place towards the end of the 18th century when King Ngwane III led his followers – mainly members of the Dlamini clan – across the Lebombo Mountains from southern Mozambique and established a capital, Lobamba, on the northern bank of the Pongola River in what is the present-day kingdom of Swaziland.

Lobamba is still regarded as the birthplace of the Swazi nation, the wellspring of the 'true Swazi', and those who trace their lineage back to this small group of Ngwane's followers still proudly refer to themselves as bakaNgwane, 'the people of Ngwane', and to their nation as kaNgwane, 'the country of Ngwane'.

Ngwane was succeeded by his son, Ndvungunya, and then by his grandson, Sobhuza I, but these men ruled in dangerous times. The early 19th century was the period of Zulu expansionism, often referred to as the Difaqane – meaning 'forced migration' – when Zulu regiments under the control of Shaka raided the countryside, establishing his hegemony over an entire region.

Both Ndvungunya and Sobhuza I ruled their subjects with an iron hand. It was Ndvungunya, for example, who set about establishing the great Swazi army and it was Sobhuza I who subsequently used it with notable success, subjugating, in his turn, a number of neighbouring peoples.

Right Even early depictions of the great Shaka alluded to the military prowess and physical strength of the famed Zulu king.

Did you know?

About 160 years ago, the Sudwala Caves – first occupied nearly two million years ago – provided the backdrop to a violent and bloody power struggle that helped forge the Swazi nation.

During the reign of Sobhuza I, the most powerful group south of the Pongola was the Ndwandwe, led by the formidable Zwide, and when Zwide turned his attention northwards, Sobhuza – realising that resistance was out of the question – led his followers north and away from danger. This migration took Sobhuza and his people along the edge of the western mountains and eventually into west-central Swaziland, where a number of defensible caves could provide sanctuary in time of danger. With what was effectively an army of occupation, Sobhuza established a new power base in the region of the Mdzimba mountains and named his new capital Lobamba (now referred to as Old Lebomba to distinguish it from the present royal residence, which was established many years later.)

It is important to remember, however, that Sobuza I was not only a fierce warrior, but also an extremely skilled diplomat. To maintain his position, for example, he took one of Zwide's daughters as his principal wife and sent two of his own daughters to Shaka as concubines. By establishing alliances and avoiding conflict in this way, this wise leader managed to maintain a fairly uneasy peace in his kingdom. Later, when Dingane – Shaka's own brother, murderer and successor – invaded the area, Sobhuza chose to retreat into the hills rather than resist the marauding invaders, and it was only in 1838 that he took on – and, indeed, overpowered – an attacking force belonging to Dingane, who was then reeling from defeat at the hands of the Boers at the Battle of Blood River.

Mswati and Somcumba

Just before his death in 1839, Sobhuza sent his sons Mswati and Somcumba back to the Lowveld-Swaziland area to establish new Swazi royal kraals, but this reconstruction had only been in progress for a few months when Sobhuza died, leaving the throne empty. Although Sobhuza had already chosen his younger son, Mswati, as his successor, the young man had not yet completed his initiation so his elder stepbrother, Somcumba, was appointed regent in his place.

The intention was that Somcumba would hand back rule to Mswati at the appropriate time, but inevitably almost, Somcumba reneged on this decision, choosing instead to hold onto

Below The kingdom of Swaziland was established through a series of migrations made by various peoples across the hinterland of southern Africa.

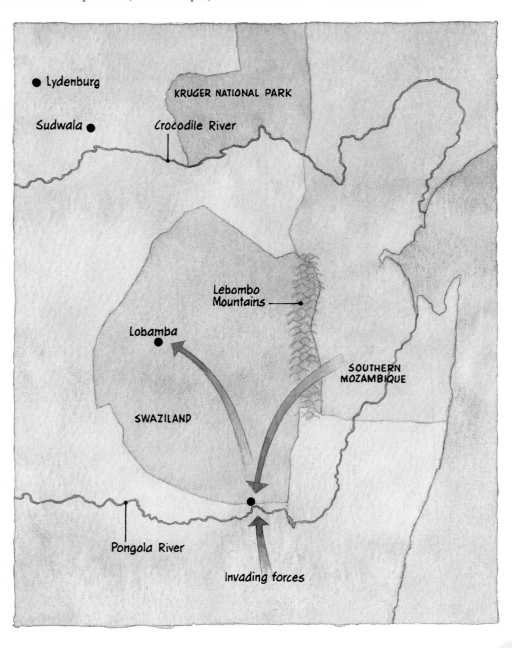

Lydenburg

KRUGER NATIONAL PARK

Sudwala

Crocodile River

Lebombo Mountains

Lobamba

SOUTHERN MOZAMBIQUE

SWAZILAND

Pongola River

Invading forces

Above Mswati's forces attempted to smoke Somcumba out of the caves where he and his men had taken refuge.

kingship when Mswati came of age. It was, thus, this decision that carved a deep schism between the Swazi people. One faction favoured Mswati, believing that as Sobhuza's chosen successor, he alone had the divine right to call himself king, while a second faction supported his stepbrother Somcumba, whom they felt would make a better king than his younger brother.

In the ensuing conflict, Somcumba and his supporters were driven out of Swaziland and into the Lydenburg area, where they established a kraal – Zondwago – on the banks of the Msilezi River (Stat River), close to Sudwala, which was both easily defensible and had ample supplies of fresh water.

When, shortly afterwards, news reached Somcumba that Mswati and his warriors were advancing on Zondwago, he immediately made the decision to retreat into the cave and, taking with them food, supplies and an entire herd of cattle, Somcumba and his followers prepared themselves for a lengthy siege.

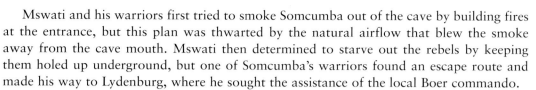

Mswati and his warriors first tried to smoke Somcumba out of the cave by building fires at the entrance, but this plan was thwarted by the natural airflow that blew the smoke away from the cave mouth. Mswati then determined to starve out the rebels by keeping them holed up underground, but one of Somcumba's warriors found an escape route and made his way to Lydenburg, where he sought the assistance of the local Boer commando.

At this stage, the Boers favoured Somcumba rather than Mswati because they believed that he (Somcumba) was partially responsible for the death of the Zulu warmonger Dingane and so it was with the help of the Boers that Mswati was chased back to the eastern banks of the Crocodile River – with considerable loss of life on both sides.

Following this incident, both Somcumba and Mswati competed for Boer support, both parties accusing the other of cattle theft, but the situation was finally resolved early one January morning when Mswati and his warriors crossed the Crocodile River and again attacked Zondwago. Somcumba was mortally wounded during the battle and there was wholesale slaughter of his supporters, the only survivor being one of Somcumba's sons, who had been running an errand for his father at the time.

After the fighting had ended, Somcumba's head was presented to Mswati – despite the fact that he had given clear instructions that his stepbrother was not to be harmed. Clearly upset that his orders had not been followed, Mswati summoned his *indunas*, and the man responsible was summarily executed – the justification allegedly being that if the warrior had killed one Swazi king, he could surely kill another.

Following the successful defeat of Somcumba, the young Mswati was firmly established as king and in the years that followed he earned for a reputation as the fiercest and, some say, the greatest of Swaziland's fighting kings. By the time of his death in 1865, the kingdom we now call Swaziland was secure, arguably as a direct result of Mswati's decisive and, indeed, forceful leadership of the Swazi people.

The natural wonders of Sudwala

Surrounded by Mpumalanga's rugged mountain slopes – in turn, cloaked in evergreen vegetation – the caves that are the focal point of Sudwala comprise a network of elaborate passages and chambers that have yet to be explored in their entirety. The Gothic interior, stretching some 30 kilometres into the mountainside, is filled with Gargoyle-like dripstone formations in hues of cream, gold, red and brown that line the interlinked caverns. These limestone stalactites formed as a result of calcium deposits, eventually meeting with the stalagmites created from the dripping, mineral-rich water on the floor of the caves to create the spectacular 'pillars' or columns for which Sudwala is famed. One of the most remarkable of these is the stalactite Somcuba's Gong (named after the legendary pretender to the Swazi throne), a cylindrical formation that echoes through the cave complex when struck. Another extraordinary feature of this network is the magnificent chamber of the P R Owen Hall, which is of mammoth proportions, with astounding acoustics that lends itself well to music concerts.

Little evidence of the excavations remains within the caves, and there is no tangible sign of its earliest inhabitants – or even of the famed Swazi fugitive. Visitors are allowed to explore only the first 600 metres of the cave system, and the Sudwala Caves remain one of South Africa's least disturbed sites of cultural, historical and natural significance.

In the name of a cave

The actual origin of the caves' name remains uncertain. Possibly, the word *sudwala* was first spelt *sidwaba*, which in Swazi means 'the grass skirt (or reed skirt) of a married woman'. However, the most likely explanation is that Sudwala was one of Mswati's warriors who was left to guard the entrance to the cave system.

Another account suggests that Sudwala was the name of one of Somcumba's supporters who took refuge in the caves following the surprise attack by Mswati. It was Sudwala, according to this version, who showed the first Europeans to visit the area the wonders of the cave, and after whom the caves are named.

The wreck of the *Haerlem*

It is against a backdrop of turbulent and unpredictable politics and a scramble for control over all-important trade routes that European merchants and adventurers sought a sea route to the Far East by which they could continue the highly lucrative overland trade that had begun almost three centuries earlier. But it was not until 1497 that Vasco da Gama finally managed to reach Calicut (now Kozhikode) on the west coast of India by sailing around the Cape of Storms, which he promptly renamed the Cape of Good Hope. The sea route to the Far East was at last opened up, but the voyage around Africa was not without its perils…

Around the Cape…

For the all-powerful Dutch East India Company, trade with the Far East was extremely profitable, but it was also extremely hazardous for the ships and men involved. The voyage from Holland to Batavia took on average about six months, and midway on this journey all drinking water on board had gone off, all fresh food had been consumed and both the salt-beef and 'hard tack' or ship's biscuit were more or less inedible. As a result, many of the

Below Even seafaring explorers of as long ago as the 1600s boasted extraordinarily accurate maps of Africa, and indeed much of the New World.

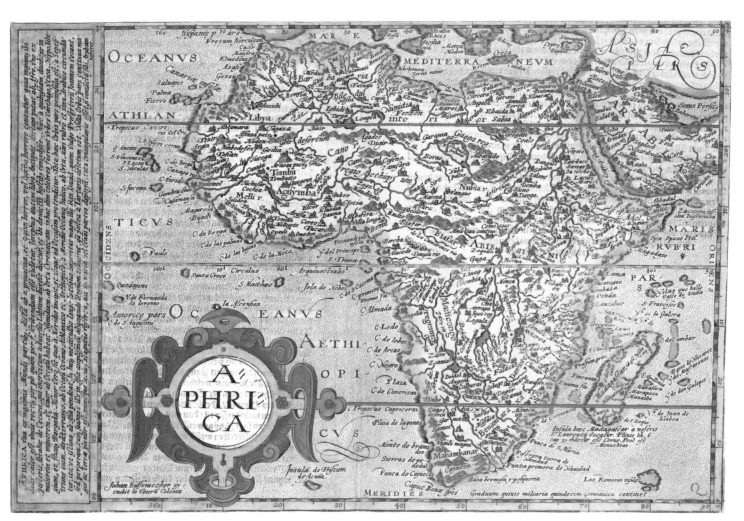

ships that arrived in the southern Atlantic were badly in need of replenishment and repair, and their crews were often dead or dying from a combination of sicknesses, including scurvy, dysentery and 'the worms'.

It was thus essential that a halfway station be established somewhere on the southern African coast where sick crewmen could be hospitalised, fresh food obtained and ships cleaned, careened and repaired, but the question was where to establish it. One possible location was Table Bay, named by Joris van Spilbergen when he had replenished there in 1601.

'This bay,' it was noted in a report written at the time, 'lying 34 degrees 4 minutes and about 15 miles north of the Cap de bon Esperance, was named the Table Bay by our General, by reason of the high hill, flat above and square like a table, and visible for 9 or 10 miles to seaward, whereby the said bay is recognised: also the ships that come to refresh there usually come to the roads below it. This Bay is very convenient for all ships to anchor, since they can do so close to land in up to four fathoms, without being exposed to much bad weather or storms... About half a mile from the Bay, eastwards of the Cap de bon Esperance, there is a creek or river extending inland where we took a good quantity of fish, in shape like carps and very tasty. Along these coasts at this season, that is in October, November and December, there blow steady south winds, as fierce and cold as the north-east winds in Holland.

'As regards the land of the Cap de bon Esperance, it is very healthy and temperate, very convenient for cultivation and habitation and for producing all manner of crops; and although it seems to be somewhat mountainous and hilly, it is also adorned with very beautiful side valleys... where the deer and roes are seen grazing and multiplying in herds... Furthermore, it is well favoured with good water from the hills... as also with animals such as oxen and sheep. As regards the people of the Cap de bon Esperance, they are yellowish in colour like *mulattoes*, very ugly of countenance, of middling stature, lean and thin of body, and very fast runners, having a very strange speech, clucking like turkeys. Their clothing is the skins of deer or other animals, worn like cloaks.'[5]

Despite this fairly encouraging report, however, no effort was made to establish a replenishment settlement of any kind at the Cape for over fifty years, and even then the site was selected quite by accident...

The *Haerlem* runs aground

The Dutch East India vessel *Haerlem* sailed out of Batavia in the company of the *Schiedam* on 22 December 1646 and was the first to arrive in Table Bay on 22 March 1647. In his diary of the events that followed, Leendert Janszen, an officer on the ship, describes how disaster struck three days later:

'After midday there came a stiff topsail-breeze from the [southeast] veering to the East... we put the helm over to leeward, but the ship refused to answer the helm, and sailing fast we neared the shore, and the sea drove us heavily... so that we ran aground. At once the ship began to pound very terribly so that all expected to be wrecked. We let fall an anchor forward in order not to be driven further aground, but the cable was broken by the great force of the surf...'

Another Dutch East India vessel, the *Elephant* attempted to give assistance, but this proved futile and shortly afterwards the captain of the *Haerlem* gave orders to abandon ship. Only one man drowned when a boat capsized and the rest of the crew managed to reach shore safely.

With the assistance of two English vessels that had arrived on the scene, most of the *Haerlem's* cargo was transferred to the *Elephant*, and it was then resolved that 'the skipper

Did you know?

The first European settlement at the Cape of Good Hope occurred by accident, or more accurately, as the result of a shipwreck.

Above More than 60 Dutch sailors lived for more than a year at Fort Sandenburgh on the Table Bay coast – well before the much-touted arrival of Jan van Riebeeck.

Hendrik Eijckens and the Chief Mate Con Wallis should leave for the fatherland, and that I [Janszen] should remain here with the Chief Mate Claes Winckels and 60 other men, to salvage as much of the Company's goods as possible'.[6]

With the help of some of the men of the *Elephant* and the *Schiedam*, the crew of the *Haerlem* set to work on building a four-sided fort, which they named Sandenburgh, on a nearby sand dune. Here they erected tents using wooden supports stretched across with tarred sails for themselves and the goods – including seeds and tools – they had managed to salvage from the doomed vessel.

Befriending the 'natives'

By 10 May, Janszen noted in his diary, the *Haerlem* had been so pounded by the waves it was nothing more than 'a complete wreck' but, fortunately for the castaways, they were able to barter meat from the locals and were, on the whole it seems, quite comfortable, though few had any wish to remain there in the long term. In a letter delivered to Holland by the *Witte Duijve*, which had stopped at Table Bay in early January 1648, for example, Janszen

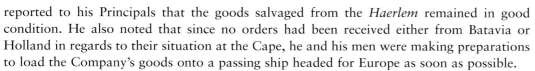

reported to his Principals that the goods salvaged from the *Haerlem* remained in good condition. He also noted that since no orders had been received either from Batavia or Holland in regards to their situation at the Cape, he and his men were making preparations to load the Company's goods onto a passing ship headed for Europe as soon as possible.

A second letter sent by Janszen with the *Witte Duijve's* sister ship, *Princess Roijael*, which arrived in Table Bay on 14 January, made reference to the fact that he [Janszen] had requested the skipper of the *Princess Roijael* to assist with the transport of the *Haerlem's* salvaged goods from Fort Sandenburgh to Salt River, but that this request had not been complied with because of 'the great weakness' of the [*Princess Roijael's*] crew.

In all, the shipwrecked crew of the *Haerlem* remained at the Cape for over a year and, and were able to raise crops, including citrus fruits, and barter with the local people, whom they called Hottentots, obtaining sheep and cattle. In the meanwhile, the goods that had been salvaged from the ship were eventually loaded onto a fleet of 12 ships that had stopped at the Cape en route for Holland in March 1648. One of the vessels in this fleet, the *Coninck van Polen*, had as a member of its crew one Jan van Riebeeck, who was returning to Europe in disgrace after being dismissed from the Company when, in charge of the Company trading station at Tongking (Tonkin, now in Vietnam), he had been found guilty of conducting private trade.

A settlement at the Cape

Back in Europe, Leendert Janszen and Matthijs Proot, who had been aboard one of the ships that rescued the Table Bay survivors, submitted a 'remonstrance' to the powers-that-be within the Dutch East India Company, recommending the establishment of a permanent replenishing station at the Cape of Good Hope. The document was balanced and well argued and painted a rather attractive picture of the Cape.

'The soil in the said [Table] valley is very good and fruitful, and in the dry season all the water one could wish for could be led through the gardens with little toil. Everything will grow there as well as anywhere in the world, especially pumpkins, watermelons, cabbages, carrots, radishes, turnips, onions, garlic and all sorts of vegetables (as those of the shipwrecked *Haerlem* found to be the case, and can testify to it).

'...Daily experience teaches us what can be done at the Cape, both for the sick and fit of the crews of the ships bound for the Indies, [even] with little sorrel and sometimes two or three cattle.

'...Since everything is to be had there in sufficient quantity, abundance of fish... further

The scourge of scurvy

Although there was a measure of understanding even in early seafaring days that fresh fruit and vegetables were an essential part of a healthy diet, this was, in effect, a moot point since there was no way of preventing fresh food from deteriorating on board ship. As a result, despite the most valiant measures to avoid the dreaded affliction, scurvy plagued a vast number of these early travellers. Not surprisingly, the death rate on long sea voyages was quite simply staggering – sometimes nearly half the crew losing their lives, a mortality rate that was by no means out of the ordinary.

Scurvy is caused by a dietary lack of vitamin C (ascorbic acid), which can be obtained from vegetables and fresh fruits, citrus fruits in particular. Although this disease has probably existed since time immemorial, the first documented cases appear in the records of the medieval crusades. However, during the latter 1400s the disease became a leading cause of sickness and death among the sailors who ventured on the long sea voyages from Europe to the Far East.

Symptoms include swollen and even bleeding gums, loosened teeth, soreness and stiffness of the joints and lower extremities, bleeding under the skin and in the deep tissues, slow wound healing, anaemia and, finally, death. Even in extremely severe cases, however, a dose of 100 milligrams of vitamin C will effect a cure within a few days.

The physician credited with the discovery of a cure for scurvy is the British naval surgeon James Lind who was the first to recommend that fresh citrus fruit and lemon juice be included in the diet of seamen. His *Treatise on Scurvy* was published in 1754 and this was followed three years later with *On the Most Effectual Means of Preserving Health of Seamen*, but it was only in 1795 that the British Royal Navy finally adopted his recommendations. As a result of this decision, scurvy was eradicated from the Royal Navy. (It also led to British sailors being referred to as 'limeys'.)

James Lind also recommended shipboard delousing procedures, the use of hospital ships and the shipboard distillation of seawater for drinking and, as a result, the good doctor is still sometimes referred to as the 'founder of naval hygiene in England'.

the elands and steenboks are abundant... There are all sorts of birds there in thousands... As some seasons of the year there is a quality of whales, and on the Robben and other islands there are always hundreds of seals... Behind the slopes of the Table Mountain there is [fire] wood enough available...'

This report also demolished the long-held myth that the locals at the Cape were savage and dangerous and in the habit of attacking Europeans for no reason. The truth was that the rare attacks had been justified and had been made in reprisal for theft or injustice on the part of the settlers...

'Others will say that the natives are brutish and cannibals, from whom nothing good is to be expected, and that we shall have to be on our guard continually; but this is only a sailor's yarn as shall be more closely shown and denied. It is not to be denied that they are without laws or government like many Indians, and it is indeed true that also some sailors and soldiers have been killed by them; but the reason for this is always left unspoken by our folk, to excuse themselves from having been the cause of it, since we firmly believe that the peasants of this country [Holland], if their cattle were to be shot down and taken off without payment, would not show themselves a whit better than these natives, had they not to fear the law.

'We of the aforesaid *Haerlem* testify entirely to the contrary as regards this since the natives, after we had been there for about five months, came daily to the fort (which we had thrown up for our defence) with all friendliness to barter, and brought cattle and sheep in quantities, so that when the ship the *Princess Roijael* arrived there with 80 or 100 sick, we so provided her with the cattle and sheep which we had in hand, and birds which they shot daily, that most of her sick again became fit, so that this refreshing was, next to God, the salvation of the ship the *Princess Roijael* and of her crew.

'Also on one occasion the Chief Mate, the Carpenter and the Corporal of the aforesaid ship *Haerlem* went as far as the place where the houses of the natives stood, and were amicably received and entertained by the said natives, who could readily have killed them when in their hands, had they been inclined to cannibalism (as is asserted by some), so that without any doubt the killing of our folk is rather in revenge for the taking of their cattle, than for eating them.

'Thus the fault is not on the side of the natives, but lies in the uncivilised and ungrateful conduct of our folk: since last year when the fleet under the command of The Hon. Wollebrant Gelijnsz already mentioned was lying at the Cape, instead of giving the natives any reward for the good treatment shown to those of the ship *Haerlem*, seven or eight of their cattle were shot down and taken off without payment, which may well cost the lives of some of our folk (if the opportunity should arise)...

'If the proposed fort is provided with a good commander, treating the natives with kindness, and gratefully paying for everything bartered from them, and entreating some of them with stomach-fulls of peas or beans (which they are greatly partial to), then nothing whatever would need to be feared...'[7]

Below Following their colonisation of the subcontinent, Dutch settlers and traders left behind a legacy of fine craftsmanship still seen in many of the ceramic pieces that survive the era.

Settlers step ashore

Jan van Riebeeck, who had spent three weeks at the Cape while the cargo and crew of the *Haerlem* were being readied to return to Holland and had been much impressed by what he had seen, volunteered to lead an expedition to establish the settlement suggested by Janszen and Proot. He was subsequently invited to comment on the document, which he did in great detail, and was appointed by the Company to set up a way station at Table Bay.

An expedition was put together and eventually a fleet of three ships, led by the *Drommedaris*, arrived in Table Bay on 6 April 1652. The fleet consisted of 200 persons, and of the 90 who were to stay at the Cape while the rest continued on to Batavia, only about half a dozen were women. This had been a conscious decision by the Company, which had no intention of setting up a permanent settlement. The objective of the exercise was merely to establish a base, which facilitated trade with the East. The rest, as they say, is history...

Above Dutch commander Jan van Riebeeck sets foot on the shores of Table Bay in April 1652, paving the way for European colonisation of southern Africa.

The *Birkenhead*: Women and children first

In January 1852, when the HMS *Birkenhead* left Cork in southern Ireland and headed south to Simon's Town, Great Britain was engaged in the so-called Eighth Frontier War. Fighting was taking place in and around the eastern border of Cape Colony and reinforcements had been called for. The conflict had proved to be a huge drain on the army's resources, and so the ship carried a full complement of military officers and men from virtually every British regiment then serving in South Africa.

A number of the troops were accompanied by their wives and children, so in addition to the military personnel on board the HMS *Birkenhead*, there were 31 children, 25 women, 125 crew, and various military and naval officers, making a total of 693 passengers. The ship also carried 250 000 gold sovereigns, which were to pay the troops while they were serving in South Africa.

The final voyage

After seven weeks at sea, the *Birkenhead* reached Simon's Town on 23 February, where she remained in dock for three days while she took on fresh water and supplies and 350 tons of coal. Once she had been fully replenished and with her decks loaded with horses and bales of hay, the *Birkenhead* set sail again at six o'clock on the evening of 26 February. She left harbour carrying 638 men, women and children; her destination – Algoa Bay, where troops from the 12th, 74th and 91st regiments were to be disembarked. After that she was to proceed to the Buffalo River where the remaining troops – those from the 12th Lancers, the 2nd, 6th, 45th and 73rd Foot, the 43rd Light Infantry and a detachment from the 60th Rifles – were to be put ashore.

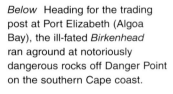

Below Heading for the trading post at Port Elizabeth (Algoa Bay), the ill-fated *Birkenhead* ran aground at notoriously dangerous rocks off Danger Point on the southern Cape coast.

BIRKENHEAD, CARRYING TROOPS FOR THE EASTERN FRONTIER, EXPECTED AT PORT ELIZABETH

PORT ELIZABETH

FROM IRELAND

SIMONSTOWN

DANGER POINT

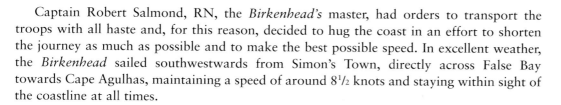

Captain Robert Salmond, RN, the *Birkenhead's* master, had orders to transport the troops with all haste and, for this reason, decided to hug the coast in an effort to shorten the journey as much as possible and to make the best possible speed. In excellent weather, the *Birkenhead* sailed southwestwards from Simon's Town, directly across False Bay towards Cape Agulhas, maintaining a speed of around 8½ knots and staying within sight of the coastline at all times.

Mayday!

Disaster struck under a clear, starlit sky at 1 am the following morning when a violent shudder shook the ship as it suddenly collided at full speed with an uncharted reef some two miles off the coast at a place called Danger Point. The collision, which tore a large gash in the hull, sent water flooding into the forward compartment and lower troop deck. At least 100 soldiers drowned in their hammocks as they slept, and the remaining passengers and crew immediately began to make their way up onto the deck.

Captain Salmond, who had also been in his cabin at the time of the collision, rushed up on deck and gave the order to 'stop engines'. He then addressed 2nd Officer Davies, who had been in charge of the bridge at the time of the collision.

'How was the light bearing when you last saw it?' he asked.

Davies said that he thought it was 'odd where it was'.

Captain Salmond was referring to a lighthouse on shore, but other passengers later suggested that the 'lighthouse' Davies had seen was in all probability a bonfire that had been lit on nearby Cape Mudge as a guide to local fishing boats.

On deck, Lieutenant-Colonel Seton of the 74th Foot took charge of the situation. He commanded his officers to take their orders from Captain Salmond, who dispatched about 60 men to man the pumps, and another 60 to launch the lifeboats. Salmond also decided to attempt to reverse the ship off the reef, a manoeuvre he hoped would prevent the ship from breaking up. Unfortunately, it had the opposite effect: no sooner had the paddles started to rotate, than a second large gash was torn in the hull, flooding the engine room within seconds.

A mere 10 minutes had passed since the ship had first run aground…

The soldiers stand firm

Shortly afterwards, Captain Salmond asked Lieutenant-Colonel Seton to assemble his men on the poop deck so as to ease the weight on the bows, and Seton thus called his officers to him, stressing the importance of maintaining 'order and silence'. Thereafter, the troops were marshalled into ranks to await further orders.

Despite the terrifying situation in which the passengers and crew found themselves, however, there was virtual silence on deck. All that could be heard was the surf crashing onto the submerged reef, and the creaks and groans of the ship as it slowly began to break up.

Lieutenant John Francis Girardot, who was in command of one sergeant and 40 privates of the 43rd Light Infantry, and Ensign GA Lucas of the 73rd regiment had been on watch at the time of the collision. Lucas would later testify that: 'Nothing could exceed the order that prevailed. Every word of command could be heard plainly as on parade.'

Distress rockets were fired and the horses, blindfolded, were forced over the side and into the water, where some were attacked by sharks. The two largest lifeboats were located atop the paddle boxes on board, but this meant they first had to be hoisted on their davits, and then swung out over the side of the ship, before being lowered into the water. The task proved impossible: in one case, the ropes used to launch the lifeboat snapped, and the other refused to budge because a davit pin was rusted in place.

Did you know?

The internationally recognised expression 'women and children first' is first associated with the HMS *Birkenhead*, which sank off the South African south coast at Danger Point, near Gansbaai, in 1852.

The first boat to be lowered into the water was a cutter – a small single-masted sailing boat – and the women and children were ordered into it, although many wives refused to be separated from their husbands, and had to be physically carried into the waiting boat.

'It is not easy to imagine a more painful task,' Lucas later testified. 'This was in several cases done by main force. Tearing them from their husbands, they were carried to the bulwarks and dropped over the ship's side into the arms of the boat's crew'.

Shortly afterwards, a second cutter was launched and then a small rowing boat known as a gig, but it was probably at this point that there was a sudden, terrifying sound of tortured metal as the bow of the ship broke off. This caused the bowsprit to leap up into the air and sent the funnel crashing down onto the deck, where it landed on the paddle box, smashing the lifeboat and killing the men who were still trying to launch her. With the bows under water, the stern – with its crowded, silent ranks on the poop deck – was high out of the water, and Captain Salmond called for the men to abandon ship.

'All those that can swim, jump overboard and make for the boats,' he said.

Lieutenant-Colonel Seton, who had been joined by Captain Edward Wright of the 91st Argyllshire Highlanders and Lieutenant John Francis Giradot, immediately begged the men to stand firm or else the rush would swamp the cutter carrying the women and children. Seton, in the meanwhile, took up station at the side of the ship with drawn sword, to prevent any of the men leaping into the boat and swamping her – though this proved unnecessary as no one tried to break ranks.

With the drummers beating the drill, the men on deck remained steadfast, shaking hands and making their final farewells. Only when it was clear that the cutter carrying the women and children was a safe distance away, did the officers also shake hands. As Lucas shook Seton's hand, he said that they would meet ashore.

'I do not think we shall, Lucas,' Seton said quietly. 'I cannot swim a stroke.'

In the later enquiry, Wright described the scene: 'The order and regularity that prevailed on board, from the time the ship struck till she totally disappeared, far exceeded anything that I thought could be effected by the best discipline; and it is the more to be wondered at, seeing that most of the soldiers had been but a short time in the service. Everyone did as he was directed and there was not a murmur or a cry among them until the vessel made her final plunge'.[8]

This, in fact, occurred merely 25 minutes after the ship had first struck the reef. Without warning, the stern, which had canted up into the air as the bow had gone down, suddenly broke off and sank beneath the waves, drowning the men working the pumps below decks and throwing the hundreds of soldiers assembled onto the poop deck into the sea.

Nearby, the survivors watched in horror. The first cutter held 35 people, including the women and children, the second cutter 36 soldiers and sailors, and the gig just nine men. Only 80 people out of the ship's complement of 638 had found places in the lifeboats. When the ship went down, the mast and rigging remained protruding from the icy water and a number of men clung to this for safety. For those who could swim, it was a long way to shore in shark-infested waters.

The morning after

Some of the survivors did, however, manage to swim the two kilometres to shore, while others clung to wreckage. One of the latter was Lieutenant Girardot, who crawled ashore at a nearby beach at about seven o'clock the next morning. In the company of half a dozen other survivors, he immediately set out inland in search of help. All along the coast behind him, survivors were straggling to shore.

During the night, the trio of lifeboats had stayed as close together as possible, but in the pounding surf it had been difficult to find a safe place to land and they had been forced to remain offshore. At around 8 am, they spotted a schooner in the distance and set off in pursuit, but were unable to catch her. Dr Culhane, who was in charge of the gig, then suggested that the eight strongest rowers man his boat in order for it to make better speed. This was done and the gig set off in pursuit a second time. The two cutters, unable to keep up with the chase, thus fell behind and became separated from each other in the increasing swell. One of them was spotted two hours later by a second schooner, the *Lioness*, which immediately changed course to investigate.

With the survivors from the rescued cutter on board, the *Lioness* reached the site where the *Birkenhead* had gone down at about two o'clock in the afternoon, and found 45 parched, exhausted men were still clinging to the upper part of the foremast and yard-arm, which was projecting out of the water above the sunken wreck.

Of the 638 persons aboard the *Birkenhead* when she sailed from Simon's Town, 443 died and only 193 reached shore alive, including all the women and children, but neither Lieutenant-Colonel Seton nor Captain Salmond were among the survivors.

The aftermath

In one fell swoop, the reinforcement force meant for the Eastern Frontier had been wiped out, but despite this military setback, the episode was held up as an example of extreme heroism and discipline in the face of mortal danger. In a letter to the *London Times* on the subject, Sir William Napier wrote:

'It may be hoped that the matchless chivalry of Captain Wright and Lieutenant Girardot and the responding generous devotion of their men, who went down without a murmur rather than risk the safety of the women and children in the boats, will meet with some public honour and reward – honour for the dead as well as for the survivors for surely the occasion was great and noble, and the heroism unsurpassable in the most noble of the noblest.'[9]

Below Only 193 people, including all the women and children on board, survived the tragic sinking of the *Birkenhead*.

The King of Prussia was also allegedly so impressed by the courage and discipline shown by the men on the *Birkenhead* that he ordered the glorious story to be read on parade at the head of all his regiments. Back at the Cape, however, people were concerned with matters more prosaic, and the following appeared in the *Graham's Town Journal* on 27 March 1852:

'Lieut Girard [sic], 43rd, arrived at King William's Town today with the remainder of the ill-fated *Birkenhead* troops. There are several incidents of a most heart-rending character. Several of the poor fellows were torn off the yards and planks by sharks, which selected all the men without clothes. It is said that Major Seton had a life preserver on, and foolishly secured 300 sovereigns round his neck, and strange to say, his pistols. It is thought that the weight of these kept his head under water, and thus he perished

'The officer of the Lancers, who was saved from the *Birkenhead*, had great luck in saving 150 sovereigns, and on reaching the shore found both his horses had landed. We hear that the *Birkenhead* had water-tight compartments, but in such a rusty state that the slides could not be closed, and that all her boat tackle was rotten – so much for the boasted trim of our naval armament.'

The *Cape Monitor*[10] also went on to report that '49 bodies have washed up and buried. The body of Dr Laing was recognised having a gold watch and £18 in money upon it. 47 packages of officers' clothing have also been washed up, and are now lying at Captain Smales. It is expected that the wreck will soon break up.' But there still remained the question of the gold…

A fortune in gold…

On Monday, 29 March 1852, almost a month to the day after the *Birkenhead* went down, she was sold by public auction. The wreck itself went for £100 and the various items that had been washed up, consisting mainly of blankets and clothing, for a further £135. Little was, in fact, said of her cargo of gold coin, but this may have been because the ship was lying in at least 12 fathoms of water, which was too deep for divers at the time to reach. There has also been speculation over the years about whether or not the *Birkenhead* was indeed carrying a large quantity of gold sovereigns, despite the fact that the records of the time indicate quite clearly that she was. This was confirmed, for example, during testimony given by Mr Richard Bevan Evans, the master's assistant, to the Judge Advocate during a court martial hearing on 7 May 1852:[11]

Question: Do you know what the *Birkenhead* was carrying?
Answer: Yes. Troops, Government stores and specie [coin].
Question: Do you know how many troops?
Answer: Not exactly without looking at the records.
Question: Do you know what stores she had on board?
Answer: Yes, but not the quantity without the manifest.
Question: Do you know what specie she carried?
Answer: Yes, there were 120 boxes of species, but I cannot say except for the manifest what each or all of these boxes contained.
Question: What did they contain?
Answer: Some 10,000, some 5,000 and some less in pounds, some gold and some silver.

Of equal significance, perhaps, is the fact that 10 years after the *Birkenhead* went down, her wreck was bought for the princely sum of £2780 for the purpose of salvage, a fact reported in the *Cape Argus* on 7 June that year:

Building the *Birkenhead*

HMS *Birkenhead* was an iron-hulled paddle steamer almost 64 metres in length, with a displacement of 1918 tons. In the plans originally submitted by to the Royal Navy for approval by the John Laird shipbuilding company in Birkenhead, England, the *Vulcan* – as the ship was provisionally named – was designed to be a frigate with two 96-pounder swivel cannons, one fore and one aft, and four 68-pounder deck cannons, two to each side. However, the Royal Navy at the time had already commissioned an iron-hulled frigate named *Vulcan*, so the plans were modified: the *Vulcan* was renamed *Birkenhead*, and she was converted into a troopship capable of carrying 500 men and equipment.

The launching of the *Birkenhead* by the Marchioness of Westminster in December 1845 was duly recorded in the *Illustrated London News* on Saturday 24 January 1846 by a somewhat overly enthusiastic shipping reporter:

'She is in fact all that can be desired by the most critical judges in naval architecture, sharpe at both extremities, yet with that fullness and rotundity of bottom and bearings which will enable her to do her work well, "blow high, or blow low".'[12]

The *Birkenhead* was, in fact, a perfect example of the transition from wind to steam power on the open sea. It had a funnel, two steam-driven six-metre side paddles and three masts: a foremast and a fore and aft mainmast.

THE WRECKED STEAMER BIRKENHEAD – It is understood that a company in England has recently purchased this steamer, as she now lies submerged near Cape L'Agulhas, for 2780 pounds; and that a number of artisans may shortly be expected to arrive for the purpose, if possible, of raising her. It will be in the recollection of many that at the time of the melancholy disaster – about 10 years ago – she went down with a considerable amount of specie on board, and was then sold by public auction for 50 pounds to two gentlemen, who have since transferred their interest in her to the above company.

Ensign Lucas, the officer of the watch when the ship ran aground, also formed the first 'Birkenhead Syndicate' in 1893 with a view to recovering the gold coin that the ship was carrying. It is clear, then, that over the years there have been a number of people keenly interested in recovering the gold on board the *Birkenhead*. The question is, did any of them achieve their objective?

Salvaging the *Birkenhead*

Arguably the most exhaustive salvage operation of the *Birkenhead* was carried out in the mid-1980s by a team of five divers led by Dr Allan Kayle. Although Kayle and his team would have liked to recover the fortune in gold coin the ship had been carrying when it went down, their objective was mainly to conduct a full archaeological survey and recovery of the wreck, with special emphasis on both cultural and historical aspects.

One must remember that a number of formal salvage operations involving the wreck have been conducted over the years, especially since the 1950s, and that the wreck has been visited by possibly hundreds of private divers during this time, so there is a chance that the gold in question has been found or removed – although there is no evidence to suggest that this has happened. Whether or not a salvager or treasure hunter would have reported such a find is debatable, but it is unlikely that it would have been possible to keep a discovery of this magnitude under wraps.

Dr Kayle's salvage operation is comprehensively described in his book *Salvage of the Birkenhead*,[13] where he reveals how, over a period of three summers from 1986 to 1989, he and his team excavated the wreck literally from stem to stern and their efforts were richly rewarded in terms of the large number of artefacts – including a few gold and silver coins – they brought to the surface, but they did not find the 120 boxes of specie referred to in the ship's manifest. (The artefacts were later distributed between Britain and South Africa, and were divided up among museums designated by the two governments.)

Does that mean that millions of Rand in gold and silver coin still lie on the seabed in fairly shallow water off Danger Point near Gansbaai? The simple answer is probably, yes. But finding it, and bringing it to the surface, remains another matter entirely!

The *Oceanos*: Captain and crew first

Many lives have been lost at sea due to negligence, bad weather, incompetence or a even combination of all of these factors, but the history books are also filled with acts of heroism and bravery carried out by captain and crew while a ship is sinking beneath them. There is no doubt that, in the vast majority of cases, the crew of a sinking vessel show great courage in time of danger. But not always. The case of the Greek cruise liner *Oceanos*, which sank off the South African coast near East London in August 1991, for example, is one exception to this noble tradition. In this instance, it was not the captain or crew who displayed bravery and fortitude in time of mortal danger, but the passengers themselves…

The party begins

Below Most of the passengers and crew aboard the *Oceanos* cruise liner were airlifted to safety one by one by helicopters of the South African Air Force.

The cruise liner *Oceanos* was built in 1952 and had previously sailed under the names of *Jean LaBorde*, *Mykinai*, *Ascona* and *Eastern Princess*. She had been renamed *Oceanos* in 1978 and was owned by the Epirotiki Steamship & Navigation Company of Piraeus, Greece.

In 1991, she was cruising South African waters on charter to TFC, a South African travel company. At around 7 pm on the evening of Saturday, 3 August, the *Oceanos* left East London for Durban on a so-called overnight 'booze cruise' with 374 passengers, 180 crew, led by Captain Yannis Avranas, and 26 TFC personnel: a total of 580 people. She was due to arrive in Durban at about 7 am the following morning. But, despite the festive mood on board, the weather was stormy, with heavy seas, strong winds gusting up to 140 kilometres per hour and eight-metre swells.

From dancing to drama

Four and a half hours after leaving port, the *Oceanos* sent out its first SOS call: the ship was taking on water, was listing to starboard and the engine room had flooded. Immediately after the distress call was received on shore, three merchant vessels in the area changed course, and three more ships – including a Portnet tug – left Durban harbour to render assistance. On shore, an alert went out to the South African Air Force and a squadron of helicopters was prepared for a rescue mission.

On board the *Oceanos* the first hint of trouble had occurred at about 9.30 pm, when most of the passengers were in the main lounge waiting for the cabaret to begin. Suddenly the lights went out and the engines stopped. Not long afterwards, the ship slowly started to list to starboard.

The passengers were informed that a hole had been discovered in the hull, but that it had been sealed off. Shortly afterwards, however, life jackets were handed out. Cruise director and master of ceremonies, Robin Boltman, said that the power supply failed just as he was about to step out onto the stage.

'The ship was plunged into complete darkness before the emergency lighting system began operating. We gathered all the passengers in the lounge and we entertainers went about calming them. We sang songs, told jokes, played musical instruments – anything to keep them calm. By this time, sea water was ankle deep on the carpets below decks. We decided to keep the passengers in the lounge and TFC Tours representative Lorraine Betts and I went below to fetch essential items such as medication for the passengers.

'The ship developed a steep list to starboard, and at about 2 am we started to lower the lifeboats. Unfortunately, due to the ship's list, we were only able to get two lifeboats away,' he said.[14]

Did you know?

In 1991, the captain of the cruise ship *Oceanos* and some of his crew abandoned the ship's passengers and were among the first to leave the sinking vessel.

These boats were filled with children and the elderly and, allegedly, some of the crew, who according to one passenger, 'pushed women and children aside in a mad scramble for the lifeboats'.[15] Not long after the boats had left, Robin Boltman went up to the bridge, and found it deserted, but managed to contact the rescue operation already started by the navy and air force.

A night of 'pure hell'

With the ship slowly sinking deeper and deeper into the water, it was a terrifying night.

'All night we clung to anything stable,' said a Mr Kotze, one of the passengers. 'Every time the boat lurched, we fell against each other and objects went hurtling past... It was a very long night of sheer terror, but people were amazingly calm. No one cried or screamed or went hysterical,' he said.

Kotze's view was echoed by Eugene Sweetman of East London: 'It was horrendous. Pure hell. Like a scene from [the popular movie] *The Poseidon Adventure*. The deck was at such a scary angle I was clinging to the railing for my life.'

The first aircraft to arrive on the scene was a C160 Hercules from Waterkloof air base, which flew over the drifting liner at 5 am. It was still dark and the deck lights on the *Oceanos* were still burning, though the ship was keeled over alarmingly. Circling the stricken vessel were a number of merchant ships, which were scouring the stormy surface of the sea with their powerful searchlights.

The captain's call

At 7.30 am, with the C160 still circling the sinking ship, 11 Puma helicopters, two Alhouette helicopters and two Dakotas arrived from Ysterplaat, Durban and Swartkops air bases. By this time, the *Oceanos* was clearly going down bow first and the remaining people still on board had scrambled up the rear deck. All the other passengers had managed to climb into the lifeboats and some had even leapt into the water in fear of the ship capsizing. All those who abandoned ship before the helicopters arrived were picked up by one of the five merchant ships circling in the area and, buffeted by 35-knot winds and operating in extremely difficult conditions, the helicopters

A world favourite

South Africa, with its moderate climate, scenic splendour, generous hospitality, and a high profile as one of the world's top wildlife destinations, currently enjoys growing acclaim in the international holiday and tourism industry and, especially after September 11, has a new-found status as one of the safest destinations in the world.[16]

- According to the World Trade Organisation, South Africa has moved up from the 52nd most popular destination in the early 1990s to 25th in 2002. (*Business Report*, 6 August 2002)

- In an informal Master Currency study, more than 85% of tourists said they were happy with the value for money in South Africa, mentioning the hospitality, scenery, good service, vacation and business possibilities, good food, shopping and friendly people. (*Business Day*, 3 December 2001)

- South African Airways (SAA) has recently received numerous awards, namely the Best Airline Award (awarded by local travel agents), the Best International Online Airline Award (rating airlines' Internet booking systems), the Best Airline to Africa Award (from the Association of British Travel Agents for cargo services), the Best Airline in Africa (from Skytrax), the Best Cabin Crew in Africa Award and, for the 11th consecutive year, the Best Airline to Africa Award in the Travel Weekly Globe Awards. The US magazine, *Business Traveler*, recently voted SAA The Best to Fly Business Class to Africa. (Website: http://www.proudlysa.co.za/stories/saa.html)

- For the cost of a burger, fries and a downmarket motel room in the US, Americans and other foreign visitors can stay in a four-star hotel in relative luxury in South Africa. For foreigners with hard currency in their pockets, the country is a cheap destination and more value for money than most other African destinations. Competing destinations such as Kenya and Tanzania tend to be more expensive because they charge dollar-based rates. (*Financial Mail*, 3 May 2002)

- South Africa's Tourism's Indaba 2002 was the biggest and best travel trade show ever to have been hosted on the African continent, attracting a total attendance of 7350 people, a 19% increase over attendance in 2001 (5948). Some 79 countries were represented, compared with 70 the previous year, with international delegate attendance up 11% (1316 from 1183) – not including an additional 184 members of the international media (up from 171 in 2001) and 31 VIPs. (Website: http://www.indaba-southafrica.co.za/travelnews/index.html)

proceeded to winch stranded passengers off the sinking ship, one by one. Captain Avranas, it appears, claimed a seat on the first helicopter, stating in later interviews that he could '…better direct rescue operations from the shore'. Needless to say, not everyone saw it that way and he was severely criticised for his actions.

One of the passengers, John Hicklin, for example, later remarked that although the captain stayed on the ship longer than most of the crew, he still 'disappeared pretty quickly'. 'There was a call for the captain to come to the bridge at one stage,' Hicklin added, 'but he said he would not. The lifeboats were trying to come back and he [Avranas] was called to supervise, but he just said, "I know there's a boat there, but there's nothing I can do." [The crew] were also scared, but they are paid to be scared.'[17]

The heroes of the hour

Having been virtually abandoned by captain and crew, the passengers on the *Oceanos* were now in extreme danger. Fortunately for them, however, there were TFC staff on board…

'When the helicopters arrived at first light, I stayed on the bridge while Miss Betts attended to the passengers on the pooldeck,' Boltman explained. 'Christopher Moss Hills from the band Crosstalk saw to the hoisting of those on the fore helicopter pad… Meanwhile, the ship's magician, Julian, and a few cronies launched the ship's rubber duck and did sterling work circling the *Oceanos* and picking up people who had fallen or jumped into the water in an attempt to reach the lifeboats… The passengers were fantastic – there was no panic, and although many were afraid, they remained cheerful.'[18]

After making sure that there were no longer any passengers aboard, Boltman was the last person to be lifted off the ship at around 11.30 that morning. By this time, the vessel was so deep in the water that furniture was being swept overboard by the waves. The navy then dropped divers to make one final search for any remaining people who may have been missed.

The ship finally went down about two hours later.

The follow-up

The 219 people who were airlifted from the *Oceanos* were first taken to the Haven Hotel outside Coffee Bay on what was then known as the Transkei coast in the Eastern Cape and from there were driven to East London, where they were met by anxious friends and family. A TFC representative also flew to East London from Johannesburg to arrange accommodation and clothing and their flights back home. Less conscientious efforts were made by others, however.

'I don't care what people say about me,' Captain Avaranas remarked later at a press conference. 'I am separated from my family, who were rescued by one of the other ships, and I have lost my own ship – what more do they want?'[19]

A naval enquiry held in Athens a year later blamed the sinking of the *Oceanos* on the captain and four of his officers who 'failed to take all the necessary measures' to ensure the ship's safety. It said that they were especially negligent in 'failing to stop the flooding of the power compartment'. The report also praised the remainder of the crew for the 'self-sacrifice and seamanship' they showed.

TFC tours, which had already paid out over R3 million in claims, and was still facing claims for a further R1 million, was placed under liquidation shortly before the board of enquiry issued its report, and an attorney representing TFC said that, in light of the report, the company would vigorously pursue its claim against the Epirotiki Steamship & Navigation Company.

St Lucia goes to war

In the latter half of 1942, building work was begun at Mount Tabor Base Camp on the heights above St Lucia. This radar and observation post, situated about 130 metres above sea level, had a commanding view of the Indian Ocean on one side and the waterways of St Lucia on the other. It was designed to support coastal command aircraft operating out of the northern end of Durban harbour in an area known as Congella. At the time, Allied shipping plying the South African coast had very little in the way of effective protection against German U-boat attacks.

Bring in the military

Below The St Lucia air base was established to service Catalina aircraft – often referred to as 'flying boats' – operating in the waters of the Indian Ocean.

In an effort to combat the German U-boat menace in the Indian Ocean, the Royal Air Force established 262 Squadron on 29 September 1942. The task of 262 Squadron would be to protect Allied shipping routes, primarily by conducting anti-submarine patrols along the East African coast and by providing escorts to ships sailing within their range of operation.

These aircraft were also used to search for survivors from ships sunk by German U-boats, and by reporting their location they helped many reach safety. On 28 December 1942, for example, the *Nova Scotia*, an auxiliary cruiser carrying 1000 Italian civil internees, was sunk about 50 kilometres off the coast of St Lucia by the German submarine, *U-177*. (The *U-177* was eventually sunk in the South Atlantic, west of Ascension Island by a US Liberator aircraft. Fifty of the crew died and 15 survived.)

On 1 December 1942, Flight-Sergeant S J Wood had been sent to St Lucia to build a new advance base on the eastern shores of the lake, near to the Mount Tabor observation bunker, and on 21 February the following year, 262 Squadron's first Catalina flying boats arrived in Durban, carrying out patrols five days later. Shortly thereafter, the squadron was relocated to a newly established flying base at St Lucia.

The squadron's first contact with the enemy occurred about three months later when the aircraft *Catalina J* sighted the German submarine *U-198*, under Kapitan Werner Hartman, while out on patrol and forced *U-198* to dive by dropping six 250-pound bombs around the submarine. The U-boat consequently suffered machine-gun damage to its port engine in the process and limped back to base. (The *U-198* was eventually sunk with all hands near Seychelles on 12 August 1944 by the British frigate HMS *Findhorn* and the Indian sloop HMIS *Godavari*.)

A second sortie occurred south of Madagascar on 20 August 1943, this time involving the *U-197* captained by Kapitan-Lieutenant Robert Bartels. On this occasion, it was *Catalina C* that attacked the submarine and forced it to dive, but shortly afterwards, the *U-197* resurfaced, probably as a result of damage sustained in the first bombing, and was attacked again. Following this renewed attack, the submarine dived a second time, leaving oil patches on the surface. The *U-197* was later reported missing with the loss of its entire crew of 67.

On 25 June 1943, *Catalina H* crashed shortly after take-off, killing eight of the nine crew, and the aircraft wreck can still be seen near the eastern shore of the lake, due west of Mount Tabor when lake levels are low.

Sightings off St Lucia

In November 1943, 262 Squadron, which by then was manned almost entirely by South African Air Force (SAAF) personnel, was transferred to the SAAF and renamed 35 Squadron. By this time, U-boat sightings in the area were occurring fairly regularly and on 5 July the following year, *U-859*, commanded by Korvettenkapitan Johann Jebsen, was sighted in the Indian Ocean by *Catalina C*.

Jebsen decided to fight it out with the attacking aircraft and during the subsequent exchange of fire, one German seaman was killed and three were wounded when depth charges landed near the submarine. The U-boat was forced to dive, leaving an oil slick on the surface of the sea.

(The U-859 was eventually sunk two months later on 23 September 1944 near Penang in the Straits of Malacca by the British submarine HMS *Trenchent*. Forty-seven of its crew of 67 were killed.)

The following day, a second unidentified U-boat was attacked by a Catalina from St Lucia, but that was to be the last aircraft attack on German submarines in South African waters during the war. The air-force base at St Lucia was finally abandoned on 2 February 1945 and the buildings were handed over to Durban Fortress Command. Mount Tabor Base Camp is now the only building left standing, although the ruins of the air base's barracks and workshops are still visible.

Did you know?

At least one German U-boat was sunk off the South African coast during the Second World War by Catalina flying boats based at St Lucia.

The bigger picture

The battle for supremacy of the world's major sea lanes, which was fought primarily between the German and British navies, was mainly confined to the Atlantic Ocean and in the first years of the war, German U-boat packs wreaked havoc on the shipping routes between Europe and North America.

At the outbreak of the war, the German U-boat fleet consisted of less than 60 submarines, but by 1943, this figure had leapt to about 400, of which about 110 were in the Atlantic at any one time.

In 1940, Britain lost four million tons of shipping, mainly as a result of submarine action. German operations destroyed a similar amount in 1941; then in 1942, the worst year of the war from the Allied perspective, this figure doubled to eight million tons lost. Most of these losses occurred off the east coast of the United States.

The HL *Hunley*:
The first submarine to sink an enemy ship

'The *Hunley* is to submarine warfare what the Wright Brothers' airplane is to aviation. It changed the course of history.' So says diver and historian Mark Ragan.

The HL *Hunley* was an iron 'diving torpedo boat', just under 40 feet long (12 metres), which was built by the Confederacy during the American Civil War. Named after its chief financial backer, Horace L Hunley, it was constructed in Mobile, Alabama, and transported by rail to Charleston, South Carolina, from where it began operations against Union ships in the latter half of 1863.

It operated with a crew of eight, seven of whom propelled the vessel by hand-cranking a single screw through a chain-driven flywheel. Air entered the submarine through twin snorkel tubes on the top of the vessel and navigation was by dead reckoning using a compass, with the captain occasionally peering through one of the two tiny view ports fitted to the superstructure.

In its first offensive operation against the Union frigate *New Ironsides*, it was swamped by a wave from a passing paddle steamer and only the captain, Lieutenant John Payne, survived. At the beginning of October 1863, the vessel capsized, drowning six of the crew. It was later raised from the bottom, but sank again with the loss of all hands – including Hunley himself – during a practice dive later the same month. Despite being christened 'The Murdering Machine', the HL *Hunley* was raised a second time, and subsequently made a number of unsuccessful attempts to attack enemy vessels.

The HL *Hunley* began its final mission on the evening of 17 February 1864, its target the Union sloop *Housatonic*, moored about six kilometres offshore. The plan was for the submarine to run about two metres below the surface until it neared the *Housatonic*, then to resurface just enough for the captain, Lieutenant George Dixon, to take a visual sighting before closing in to attach the vessel's primitive depth charge.

The HL *Hunley's* armament consisted of a single explosive charge fitted to the end of a long lance at the prow of the vessel. It would drive this lance into the hull of the target vessel and then withdraw to a safe distance, leaving the charge behind. The explosion was triggered using a length of cord linking the submarine to the explosive. Although the HL *Hunley* successfully sank the *Housatonic*, it was not seen again for 131 years…

In May 1995, the HL *Hunley* was discovered under three metres of silt about 1000 metres from the wreck of the *Housatonic* by a salvage team led by the novelist Clive Cussler. Following a rather lengthy salvage operation, it was eventually brought to the surface in 2000.

During this period of the war, German 'wolf packs' – where groups of up to 15 U-boats would combine to lay in wait for Allied convoys – were sinking an of average five ships a day. The problem for the Allies was twofold: many of the convoys were slow-moving and were largely unprotected as most British naval vessels, destroyers in particular, remained close to the British Isles in order to repel an anticipated German invasion. Furthermore, the Germans had also managed to break the Allied codes, which meant that they could monitor communications and often knew the size, location and destination of convoys they intended to attack. Significantly, the British and Americans were aware of this because they had also managed to break the German secret cipher system, though they acted upon this knowledge with some caution, sometimes sacrificing vessels they knew the Germans would attack, in order to protect what they saw as a tactical advantage, at least in terms of intelligence gathering.

The climax finally came in March 1943 when the Allies lost 97 ships in the first 20 days of the month. In fact, it was at this point that the situation became so critical the Allies began to use the knowledge they had obtained from deciphering the German coded transmissions in order to redirect the convoys away from the gathering wolf packs. In addition, far greater numbers of naval escort vessels were employed to protect the convoys and to attack the German wolf packs. The Allies also replaced the compromised coded message system used by their convoys so that the enemy could not decipher their ship-to-ship and ship-to-shore transmissions.

Another factor in the Allies' favour was that they had developed a revolutionary valve called a magnetron, which gave them radar capability of exceptional range and accuracy. This 'new' radar system, which was fitted to Royal Navy escorts, could locate the conning tower and sometimes even the periscope of a submarine in darkness and proved very effective. Aircraft were also being fitted with airborne radar called ASV (Air-to-surface vessel), which proved equally effective and made submarines extremely vulnerable to air attack.

As a result, within two months the tables were turned. In the first 21 days of May 1943, the Germans lost 40 U-boats and a further 72 over the following three months, 58 of these submarines destroyed in attacks from the air.

Admiral Doenitz, commander-in-chief of the German Navy's U-boat arm, ordered an immediate inquiry into the cause for these devastating losses and when it was determined that the U-boat losses were not because the Allies had broken their codes – which was, in fact, the case – he decided to disband the highly successful wolf-pack system in favour of the much less effective system of having single U-boats act independently from each other.

Even as late as 1959, when Doenitz published his memoirs, he refused to believe that the security of the German Navy's coded transmissions had been compromised in any way. He attributed the British successes to a highly superior radar system. In fact, it was the Allies' intelligence capability – in other words, the fact that they could read the German signals – rather than their technical superiority, which was arguably the most significant factor in the war for control of the seas.

The *Dodington* makes history

On 1 October 1997, South Africa's National Monuments Council (NMC) received an article published in *The Times* of London entitled 'Clive of India's Gold Found in Pirate Week' that advertised a forthcoming auction in London of 1200 gold coins, weighing a total of 620 ounces. The article also claimed that these coins were part of 653 ounces of gold Robert Clive – appointed by the directors of the British East India Company to lead its operations in India – had taken with him when he sailed for India in 1755.

The gold in question – which was part of Clive's personal fortune – plus a large quantity of silver was placed aboard the *Dodington*, which sailed from Dover on 22 April 1755 accompanied by the *Stretham*, *Pelham*, *Edgecote* and *Houghton*. Clive, who could not get a berth on the *Dodington*, sailed on the *Stretham* – and fortunate it was for him too as, due to a navigational error, the *Dodington* struck a reef off Bird Island in Algoa Bay on 17 July 1755. Of the 270 passengers and crew aboard the ship, only 23 survived, and none of the gold was recovered...

In 1977, the *Dodington* was located by David Allen and Gerry van Niekerk and five years later, following an amendment to the National Monuments Act, Allen and Van Niekerk applied for and received a permit to excavate the site in collaboration with the Port Elizabeth Museum. (In fact, it was Allen and Van Niekerk who petitioned parliament to pass laws to protect historical shipwrecks when they observed the ruthless poaching and plundering of shipwrecks off the South African coast, once word of their discovery leaked out. The final result of their efforts was the 1979 amendment to the Act.)

Did you know?

South African law currently states that any 'treasure' found on a wreck in South African waters may not be tampered with or removed without permission from the relevant authorities.

On learning – via *The Times* article – of the proposed sale of the *Dodington* coins, the National Monuments Council instituted legal proceedings against the alleged owner of the gold and silver, and the auction was cancelled, with the auctioneer, Spink & Son, retaining possession of the coins until ownership could be established. But subsequent attempts by the NMC to establish the identity of the seller proved fruitless, though acting through lawyers, the seller did say that the coins were (a) found in international waters – which was not the case since the *Dodington* went down in South African waters – and (b) that the coins were removed by pirates shortly after the ship went down, which was also considered implausible.

After four years of legal wrangling, a negotiated settlement was finally agreed upon in 2001: one third of the coins were returned to South Africa, with the rest being retained by the Florida coin dealer who claimed ownership.

So says the law...

Maritime law can be extremely complicated. This is certainly the case where shipwrecks are concerned and, to make matters worse, marine salvage can often be a murky, cloak-and-dagger world of intrigue and secrecy. In addition to these problems, there are also a number of unresolved issues concerning the legal jurisdiction and ownership of wrecks. Some divers believe that the principle of 'finders keepers' applies to shipwrecks, but this is often not the case. Legal opinion suggests that the ownership of wrecks that lie within South African waters, for example, is vested in the State, and in particular in the person of the State President, who is the representative of the nation.

Generally speaking it is undisputed that states have control over wrecks and sites found in their territorial waters, but this does not mean that the State can automatically claim ownership. The ownership of a ship found in the territorial waters of one nation is sometimes disputed by the country under whose flag the vessel originally sailed.

In 1970, for example, the Dutch vessel *Akerendam*, which sank in Norwegian waters in 1725, was salvaged and a large quantity of gold and silver coins was brought ashore. The Dutch government claimed ownership of the vessel and eventually negotiated a settlement in which it received just 10 per cent of the coins recovered.

The case of the SS *Central America*, which sank about 250 kilometres off the coast of South Carolina in the USA in 1857 is another case in point. The ship contained a large quantity of gold, some of which was recovered by the Columbus-America Recovery Group in 1988. The group then attempted to have themselves declared owner of the gold, but this was opposed by 31 British and American insurance companies, who claimed that the gold was theirs by right of the fact that they had paid out insurance to the owners at the time the ship went down. The American courts upheld this view.

Another question in the case was whether the insurance companies had 'abandoned' the property, meaning that they no longer had a claim to it because they had made no efforts to recover their property. The courts ruled that this was not the case and, in the end, Columbus-America was deemed the salvor of the wreck, and as such were entitled to 92,7 per cent of all the gold and artefacts raised from the deep.

The wreck of the *Titanic* has also raised similar issues. A Virginia court has declared that the owner of any artefacts raised from the ship are the property of RMS Titanic Inc., the salvors of the vessel – despite the fact that the *Titanic* lies hundreds of miles from American waters. It is debatable whether this court decision would hold up in a case where another salvage operator, not based in the United States, also laid claim to the wreck.

Significantly, up until 1997 the National Monuments Council had not instituted any legal proceedings against either a diver or salvor who was thought to have contravened the National Monuments Act. Part of the problem has undoubtedly been the fact that the NMC has a limited budget for legal action, but there is also the recognition that the status of cultural heritage offences within the justice system is extremely low and they are, therefore, often considered low-priority offences. Some have also argued that the NMC itself lacks confidence in the law because some of the provisions laid down in the Act are unenforceable.

The plundering of shipwrecks

Since the invention of scuba-diving equipment in the1940s, the plundering of shipwrecks around the world has been rife and this practice has now reached epidemic proportions. In South Africa, the preservation of any shipwreck that is more than 50 years old and lies within South African national waters – 24 nautical miles or 44,4 kilometres from the coast – is the responsibility of the National Monuments Council. The NMC, in turn, operates within the constraints of the National Monuments Act (1969). In principle, a function of the NMC is to protect South Africa's national heritage from those who would destroy it, accidentally or otherwise, or seek to exploit it for personal gain.

A 1979 amendment to the National Monuments Act gave the NMC the power to declare any shipwreck that fell within South African national waters a protected site. However, where this amendment fell down was that it did not make it illegal to remove the contents or cargo from a proscribed shipwreck, merely that it was an offence to interfere with the ship itself.

In 1981 a further amendment to the Act was passed, which stated that a permit issued by the NMC was required to 'destroy, damage, alter or export from the Republic' any one of a list of artefacts known to have been in the country or its territorial waters for more than 100 years. And in 1986 another amendment to the Act made it an offence to interfere with or disturb in any way a shipwreck over the age of 50 years.

What this all means is that it is now an offence to remove anything from, or disturb in any way, any shipwreck that is more than 50 years old and is located within about 44 kilometres of the South African coast without the permission of the NMC.

But having a law is one thing; enforcing it and making it work in practice is another…

Endnotes

1. The author gratefully acknowledges the kind assistance of the following individuals in the compilation of this chapter: Martin Loots, Johan Verhoef, Dr Ronald Clarke and Dean Riley-Hawkins.
2. Martin Hall, *The Changing Past – Farmers, Kings and Traders in South Africa 200–1860* (1987), Cape Town: David Philip Publishers, p. 78.
3. Ibid.
4. *Philips Atlas of Exploration* (1996), London: Philips, p. 26.
5. R Raven-Hart and R Major, *Before Van Riebeeck* (1967), Cape Town: Struik Publishers, p. 168.
6. Ibid.
7. Ibid.
8. N Mostert, *Frontiers* (1992), London: Jonathan Cape, p. 139.
9. The Royal Green Jackets Association website: www.rgjassociation.org.uk
10. Allan Kayle, *Salvage of the Birkenhead* (1990), Johannesburg: Southern Book Publishers, p. 30.
11. Ibid., p. 38.
12. Ibid., p. 5.
13. Ibid.
14. *Business Day*, 5 August 1991.
15. *The Citizen*, 5 August 1991.
16. Proud to be South African website, http://www.insanetree.com
17. *The Citizen*, op. cit.
18. *Business Day*, op. cit.
19. *The Citizen*, op. cit.

Amazing Animals

We share our world with animals and are reminded of the important role they play in our lives by nineteenth-century novelist George Eliot: 'Animals are such agreeable friends – they ask no questions, they pass no criticisms.' In most instances, however, we tend to take them for granted – except for those few, rare, special occasions when we are reminded that our lives, and the lives of the many living creatures with which we coexist, are inextricably linked. South Africa has had more than its fair share of amazing animals. Here are the stories of but a few of the more memorable individuals...

A brave horse called Boetie

On 31 May 1773, strong winds and driving rain began to lash the Cape Peninsula and, despite the Governor's decree that prohibited ships from anchoring in Table Bay during the winter months of May to October – visiting vessels were expected to sail around the peninsula to the safety of protected False Bay – five ships belonging to the Dutch East India Company lay at rest in the harbour that day. They were *Duyf en Brug*, *Aschat*, *Overhout*, the hooker *De Snelheid* and the *De Jonge Thomas*.

As the day wore on, the storm worsened. Out at sea, with the wind screaming through the rigging and with giant waves buffeting the sides of the vessels, all the passengers and crew could hope for was that the anchors would hold and that their prayers would be answered. Meanwhile, those on shore were forced to watch helplessly as the sea's fury grew with every passing hour.

Finally, at about 5am on the morning of 1 June, disaster struck. Just before dawn, the *De Jonge Thomas* broke its mooring and began drifting towards the mouth of the Salt River. In desperation, the crew of the stricken vessel raised a small sail in a futile attempt to sail out to sea, but despite their valiant efforts, wind and waves continued to drive the doomed ship closer and closer towards the rocky shore.

The storm-battered ships in the bay began firing their cannons to attract the attention of the small group of onlookers who had ridden out from the town and now stood on the beach, but there was little anyone could do other than watch the drama unfold.

And then, just as the sun began to appear on the distant horizon, *De Jonge Thomas* struck a sandbank about 500 metres from shore and immediately began to break up. Passengers, crew and cargo were flung into the rolling sea, the cries of distress from the injured and the drowning rising above the howling wind – but the mountainous seas made it too dangerous for anyone to put out from shore to help them. It was a terrifying sight and those on shore

A good horse

A good horse sholde have three propyrtees of a man, three of a woman, three of a foxe, three of a haare and three of an asse.

Of a man. Bolde, prowde and hardye

Of a woman. Fayre-breasted, fair of heere, and easy to move.

Of a foxe. A fair taylle, short eers, with a good trotte.

Of a haare. A grate eye, a dry head, and well rennynge.

Of an asse. A bygge chynn, a flat legge, and a good hoof.

— Wynkyn de Worde (1496)

Left A dairyman by trade, Wolraad Woltemade and his horse Boetie braved the waves no fewer than seven times in order to save the drowning and injured.

Did you know?

Wolraad Woltemade and his brave horse, Boetie, rescued 14 people from a sinking ship in Table Bay in 1773. The Woltemade Decoration for Bravery, South Africa's most significant honour for heroic acts of bravery, was named in special tribute to the humble dairyman.

prayed that fate would intervene and wash one or two lucky souls to safety on the beach. The chances of that happening were, however, slim indeed.

As soon as news of the stricken vessel reached the town, a contingent of soldiers was dispatched from the Castle with orders to impound any cargo washed up on the beach. On arrival at the scene, soldiers herded the onlookers away from the water's edge. It was a capital offence punishable by death, they warned the assembled crowd, to steal any cargo from the sinking vessel, and to drive home the point that punishment would be swift and merciless, they erected a temporary gibbet on the beach.

To the rescue

One man, however, refused to stand by and do nothing. His name was Wolraad Woltemade and he had ridden out to deliver breakfast to his son, a corporal in the military. The anguished cries from the passengers on the sinking ship were tearing him apart. 'Why doesn't someone help them?' he asked, but those around him just shrugged.

There was nothing anyone could do. To venture out into the swirling surf would be suicidal, and it was a risk no one was willing to take.

When Woltemade approached his son, he received the same answer.

'Our orders are only to salvage the cargo,' the young man informed him.

But the elder Woltemade was a brave man, and not one to stand by doing nothing while others suffered.

'If no one else will try to save them, I will,' he said.

Then, having made up his mind, he patted his horse on the neck. 'Come, Boetie,' he said, and headed down towards the crashing waves.

For a moment, horse and rider stood at the water's edge. Woltemade then urged his mount into the waves. In an instant, they were seized by the swirling backwash and swept out beyond the breakers. Spotting two men floating amid the flotsam and jetsam, Woltemade threw them a rope and he and the equally brave Boetie towed them back to shore. He stayed on dry land only long enough for Boetie to catch his breath, before plunging back into the water.

Seven times horse and rider returned to the raging waters that terrible morning, and seven times they dragged the drowning and injured to safety. But this superhuman effort was taking its toll. The 65-year-old Woltemade and his horse, Boetie, had saved the lives of 14 people, but both man and animal were exhausted and close to collapse themselves.

After the seventh rescue, Woltemade's son pleaded with his father to stay ashore, that he had done all that could be expected. But the old man refused to give up. Hearing renewed cries of distress, he urged his horse back towards the water once again.

'Just one more time, Boetie,' he urged. 'Just one more time.'

For the eighth time, they swam out from the beach, heading towards a section of the wreck where half a dozen men were clinging in panic to a broken spar. Seeing Woltemade and his horse draw near, the men threw themselves into the water in a last, desperate attempt to save themselves. But the weight of bodies was too much for the exhausted horse and rider and they went under, taking the panic-stricken seamen with them.

Of a complement of 207 men, women and children on *De Jonge Thomas*, 140 perished, but 14 of the 67 survivors owed their lives that day to the bravery of Wolraad Woltemade and his horse, Boetie.

Although there is no record of Boetie's corpse ever having beached following the storm, Woltemade's body was washed up the next day and he was buried without fanfare in the town shortly afterwards. To commemorate Woltemade's brave action the Dutch East India Company did, however, name one of their new vessels *De Held Woltemade*, and on its stern was a carving depicting his brave exploit.

On the battlefields

For hundreds of years, the knee-to-knee cavalry charge was a common battle tactic for most cavalry units. During the 19th century, however, it was generally recognised that this form of combat was out of step on the modern battlefield and too often resulted in unacceptably high casualty rates, both for men and horses – particularly when the cavalry faced modern

Did you know?

The setting up of the British Army Veterinary Corps in 1903 was a direct result of public outrage at the treatment of horses by the British Army during the South African (Anglo-Boer) War.

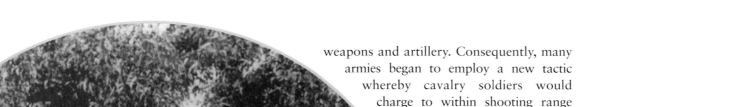

weapons and artillery. Consequently, many armies began to employ a new tactic whereby cavalry soldiers would charge to within shooting range of the enemy, dismount, fire until their ammunition was exhausted, and then leap back into the saddle and gallop to safety.

Although by the end of the 19th century the British Army was slowly beginning to treat its horses more humanely, it could be argued that these animals were still frequently abused, be it intentionally or otherwise. While it cannot be said that British commanding officers regarded their men and horses as dispensable, they did however appear willing to order subordinates to charge directly into the face of enemy guns despite the lessons that should have been learned during the so-called Charge of the Light Brigade on 25 October 1854.

In this famous action, the British Light Brigade of Cavalry attack entrenched Russian artillery during the battle of Balaclava in the Crimea, and more than a third of the British force of 673 was killed or injured during this action.

The gallop-and-dismount strategy was employed by the Boers on horseback during the South African (Anglo-Boer) War – much, it would appear, to the disdain of the British commanders. In many cases, the British remained wedded to the idea of the more old-fashioned knee-to-knee cavalry charge, despite the fact that there was often no one to charge.

The Boers' horses were tough and wiry little ponies that could live off the land, far more suited to the climate and terrain than those of the enemy, and had been trained to stand still once the reins were thrown over their heads, which made escape after a skirmish considerably easier. British horses, though arguably of 'superior' pedigree, were on the other hand unsuited to the vicissitudes of the harsh South African climate. Out of 520 000 mounts supplied to British troops during this conflict, some 326 000 died – more as a result of disease and exhaustion than enemy fire.

Such was the public outrage at the suffering and loss of equine life – and the waste of public money – during the war that a parliamentary committee was set up to look into the matter. This eventually led to formation of the Army Veterinary Corps in 1903.

According to a Royal Society for the Protection and Care of Animals (RSPCA) pamphlet published after the war, some of the worst recollections of the soldiers involved in the conflict were of the cries of pain and suffering of the injured horses, and their sorrow at having to abandon these creatures in their hour of misery.

Left Today, Durban is host to a monument commemorating the horses and mules that died during the South African (Anglo-Boer) War.

Horse power

'The power to vertically raise 33 000 lbs by one foot in one minute.'

The unit of power measurement we today call 'horse power' was first established by the famous Scottish engineer, James Watt (1736 – 1819). Watt was seeking to compare the power of the steam engines he invented with that of horses. Watt estimated that a strong dray horse working at a gin for eight hours a day, averaged 22 000 foot pounds per minute. He increased this by 50 per cent and this figure – the ability to raise 33 000 lbs by one foot in one minute – eventually became the recognised unit for measuring power.

Able Seaman Just Nuisance

The Great Dane was born in Rondebosch, Cape Town, on Thursday 1 April 1937. The lively young puppy was bought by Benjamin Chaney, who not long afterwards moved to Simon's Town – which at the time acted as a base for the Royal Navy – in order to take up a position as head of the United States Institute (USI). It is at this point that the story of Just Nuisance really begins...

Just one of the men...

Simon's Town liked Mr Chaney's Great Dane and Mr Chaney's Great Dane liked Simon's Town. In 1939, many of the USI's customers were naval ratings and most – if not all – seemed to be dog lovers. Before long, Mr Chaney's friendly dog had become a popular local celebrity and, as with all celebrities, he had his own fan club, many of whom provided him with tasty titbits or even took him for walks around the town. And it was hard for a dog not to notice that all these adoring fans seemed to wear the same uniform of blue bell-bottom trousers, square blue collars and flat-topped naval caps. Not surprisingly, Mr Chaney's Great Dane soon learnt to show considerably more enthusiasm for the company of ordinary ratings than he did for officers or women, and began following his newfound friends into the naval base and dockyards. It was here that he developed a particular fondness for HMS *Neptune*, where he would sun himself on the gangplank, occasionally to the chagrin of the crew. Being a large dog, it was sometimes difficult to sidle past him in order to board or disembark from the ship and some of the sailors were in the habit of saying, 'You're a nuisance!' when they were forced to step over him. This, so the story goes, was how people started calling Benjamin Chaney's Great Dane 'Nuisance'. And the name just seemed to stick.

Nuisance becomes unpopular

But life for Nuisance was not all plain sailing, and a dark cloud first appeared on the horizon when he began accompanying his 'sailor friends' on the train when they went into Cape Town on shore leave. To most people, the fact that they sometimes shared their journey to or from the city with an unaccompanied dog was little more than an amusing anecdote to tell their friends, but the railway authorities took a dim view of the situation. Angry and increasingly frustrated ticket collectors began putting Nuisance off the train, but this course of action proved itself singularly ineffective since Nuisance would either reenter the carriage through an open window or simply wait on the station for the next train before continuing his journey.

Below In tribute to the legendary Great Dane, a statue of Able Seaman Just Nuisance looks out over the harbour and naval base in Simon's Town where he carried out his duties.

In the face of this 'problem', exasperated railway officials began sending a stream of demands to Mr Chaney, requesting him to keep his animal under control and away from the trains. This, however, proved to be impossible and the situation eventually became so grave that the South African Railways authority warned Mr Chaney that if he did not control his animal, the dog would have to be put down.

When the ultimatum became known, there was a huge public outcry and, since Nuisance was in some respects a navy dog, the Commander-in-Chief of the Navy (South Atlantic) found himself deluged with letters of protest requesting that he intervene.

Nuisance joins the navy

After much soul-searching, the Commander-in-Chief decided to resolve the matter by officially enlisting Nuisance into the Royal Navy as an 'Ordinary Seaman'. As a 'volunteer', the dog would be entitled to all the benefits of a serving naval rating, including a free pass on the railways. Not only would this solution save the dog from a less-than-pleasant fate, it also immediately elevated him to a position where, almost overnight, he became one of the most famous dogs in the world. And thus on Friday 25 August 1939, Nuisance was taken to the recruiting office of HMS *Afrikander* where he was officially inducted into the Royal Navy. On his official application form, Nuisance's trade was described as 'Bonecrusher' and his religion as 'Scrounger', later amended to Canine Divinity League (Anti-vivisection). The only problem was that no one knew what to put in the block headed 'Christian name', and so it was that one of the men present suggested that they 'leave it out and give the name as just Nuisance', which is how Mr Chaney's Great Dane became known as (Ordinary Seaman) Just Nuisance.

To formally conclude the matter, Just Nuisance 'signed' his registration papers with a paw mark and then, like all new recruits, went for his medical examination. Having been declared 'fit for active duty', he had his name, rank and number etched into his collar and he was given a regulation seaman's cap, though one with a strap under the chin.

Just Nuisance gained a reputation for the care and consideration he showed his fellow enlistees. If two sailors began fighting in his presence, for example, he would separate the antagonists by standing on his hind legs and resting his front paws on the chest of one of

Left Able Seaman Just Nuisance, dressed for duty.

Did you know?

In 1939, a Great Dane named Just Nuisance was formally enlisted as an 'Ordinary Seaman' into the Royal Navy, based in Simon's Town.

Right Just Nuisance's size and human-like qualities ensured that he was accepted as one of the boys.

the two men, forcing both of them to stop. And on the train, he would 'help home' those sailors who showed themselves to be rather the worse for drink, even, sometimes, if the rather unfortunate inebriate didn't live in Simon's Town!

As a result of his dedicated service, Just Nuisance was soon promoted to the rank of Able Seaman, which meant that he was entitled to naval rations. He was also given his own bed and billeted in Hut Number One, where he could often be found sleeping stretched out with his head on the pillow. In addition, he began taking his meals with the other ratings, was granted shore leave every night and was assisted in his duties by a fellow seaman, who had the task of ensuring that he was washed regularly and that he appeared on parade wearing his cap.

This is not to suggest, however, that there wasn't a darker side to our hero.

Although Just Nuisance had a reputation as a kind and loving dog where humans were concerned, the same couldn't be said of other animals – dogs especially. He fought with and killed the mascots from two other ships, HMS *Redoubt* and HMS *Shropshire*, and also committed a number of other offences that were duly recorded on his Conduct Sheet. These included travelling on a train without his free pass, sleeping on a bed in the Petty Officers' dormitory, going AWOL (Absent Without Official Leave), losing his collar and resisting eviction from local pubs at closing time.

His Conduct Sheet, which is now on display at the Simon's Town Museum, shows three recorded offences:

- Travelling on the railway without a pass. Punishment awarded: Confined to the banks of Froggy Pond, Lily Pool, with all lampposts removed.
- Did sleep in an improper place, namely in a bed in the Petty Officers' dormitory. Punishment awarded: Deprived of bones for seven days.
- Did resist ejection from the Sailors' & Soldiers' home. No punishment awarded.

Military honours

Although Just Nuisance never went to sea, he did – despite regulations forbidding it – occasionally join air reconnaissance flying off the South African coast in their search for enemy submarines. However, as a 'bone-fido' local celebrity, he attended a number of fêtes and fund-raising events as the guest of honour, and when circumstances prevented him from accepting an invitation, he would always send a formal letter of apology. On one occasion, for example, he explained that: 'My C.O. informs me that my appearance might result in a flood of applications for service in the Royal Navy.' And to another admirer, who seemed to be under the impression that he was a sheep dog, he wrote: 'I'm not a sheepdog, and nor do I like sheep – except as mutton.'

Eventually, Just Nuisance lost his heart to a Great Dane bitch named Adinda and the two dogs were joined in matrimony. Five puppies resulted from this union, two of whom – Victor and Wilhelmina – were presented to the mayor of Cape Town and later auctioned for war funds. Sales of a book about him – *Just Nuisance: Able Seaman Who Leads A Dog's Life* by Leslie Steyn – as well as numerous postcards of him with his pups also raised large sums of money for the war effort.

Normally, Great Danes don't live for more than seven or eight years. Towards the end of 1943, Just Nuisance injured a leg while jumping from a moving truck and, despite receiving the best treatment available, eventually had to be invalided out of the service. His formal discharge from HMS *Afrikander*, where he had been 'stationed', took place on Monday, 1 January 1944. Three months later, on 1 April 1944 – his seventh birthday, Just Nuisance was transported to Simon's Town Naval Hospital where he was put to sleep by the naval surgeon. The following day at 11h30 his body, wrapped in a canvas bag, and covered with a white Royal Naval Ensign, was laid to rest with full military honours – including a firing party of Royal Marines and a lone bugler – at Klaver Camp on top of Red Hill, Simon's Town.

In remembrance of a truly remarkable dog, his grave was marked with a granite headstone and a bronze statue was commissioned, which now stands in Jubilee Square, Simon's Town.

Below On his death in April 1944, Able Seaman Just Nuisance was buried with full military honours on a hill overlooking his beloved Simon's Town.

Jock of the Bushveld

Arguably South Africa's most famous dog story of all time, Sir Percy Fitzpatrick's *Jock of the Bushveld* was first published in September 1907 and has remained in print ever since. Sir Percy was born on 24 July 1862 in King William's Town, the eldest son of James Coleman Fitzpatrick, judge of the Supreme Court of the Cape Colony, and was educated at Downside Abbey near Bath, England, St Aidan's College, Grahamstown and

Right and below Adding to the universal appeal of Fitzpatrick's much-loved novel was the series of fine illustrations by Edmond Caldwell in the 1907 edition published by Ad Donker.

the South African College, Cape Town. On his father's death in 1880, the young Percy left college and joined the Standard Bank, but resigned in 1884 and moved to the Eastern Transvaal where he became a storeman, prospector's hand, journalist and transport rider for six years. It was during this period of his life that he acquired his dog, Jock, and around which *Jock of the Bushveld* is based.

After Percy lost everything following a tsetse-fly outbreak that infected his oxen, he moved to Barberton in 1889, where he met Lillian Cubitt, whom he married in the same year. He later joined a mining company and became active in politics. Following the collapse of the Jameson Raid on 2 January 1896, he was arrested for high treason, and was sentenced to two years in prison and fined £2,000.

Although he was released in May of the same year, Percy was prohibited from participating in politics for a further three years, and thus returned to the mining industry, becoming a partner in Herman Eckstein & Co. His book, *The Transvaal from Within*, a personal account of public and political affairs within the Transvaal at that time, was published to much critical acclaim in 1899, immediately after the expiry of his prohibition.

Percy acted as an unofficial adviser to the British government during the South African (Anglo-Boer) War and was knighted for his efforts in 1902. He subsequently became chairman of the Chamber of Mines and contributed greatly to the setting up of the Union of South Africa.

Before moving to Johannesburg in 1889, Percy had given his dog, Jock, to a friend, who later passed him on to a trader named Tom Barnett, who kept a store just outside Maputo in Mozambique. Barnett, however, accidentally killed Jock one night after the dog had rushed out of the house to attack a stray that had invaded the henhouse. Although Jock killed the trespasser, he was mistaken for the intruder himself and shot.

Left The playful and loving nature of the beloved canine and the remarkable bond between dog and master ensured that *Jock of the Bushveld* became a literary classic, much reprinted over more than a century since it was first published.

Sir Percy was encouraged to write *Jock of the Bushveld* by his close friend Rudyard Kipling and his own children – to whom he often recounted the adventures he and Jock enjoyed during their pioneering days together in the bushveld.

Sir Percy died on 24 January 1931 and is buried at The Outlook, overlooking the Sundays River Valley. He is most acclaimed for his works, *Through Mashonaland with Pick and Pen* (1892), *The Outspan* (1897), *The Transvaal from Within* (1899) *Jock of the Bushveld* (1907), *The Origin, Causes and Objects of the War* (1914) and *Lord Milner and His Work* (1925).

Laika's story

The first artificial satellite, named *Sputnik 1*, was launched by the Soviet Union on 4 October 1957, and consisted of a spherical capsule 58 centimetres in diameter and weighing 84 kilograms. *Sputnik 1* carried only a simple radio transmitter that allowed scientists to track its progress as it orbited the earth.

On 3 November 1957, the Russians then launched *Sputnik 2*. *Sputnik 2* weighed 500 kilograms and carried the dog Laika, the first living creature to orbit the earth. Laika, who had been conditioned to accept a confined space, was strapped into an air-conditioned chamber, provided with a supply of food and water and was wired to a number of sensors so that scientists on earth could monitor her pulse and respiration. Re-entry and recovery were not possible at the time and Laika died in space when her oxygen supply eventually ran out, 10 days after launch.

The first animals to survive orbital flight were the dogs Belka and Strelka, who travelled in *Sputnik 5*, launched from the Soviet Union on 19 August 1960. Before returning to earth, *Sputnik 5* completed just over 17 orbits during a flight that lasted 25 hours. Pushinka, one of Strelka's puppies, was later presented to American First Lady, Jackie Kennedy, wife of President John F Kennedy, in 1961 by the Soviet Premier Nikita Krushchev.

Did you know?

A Russian dog named Laika was the first living creature to travel in space.

The strange story of Huberta the Hippo

The story of Huberta is one of South Africa's most endearing true-life animal tales. It begins in what was then Zululand, Natal, in late November 1928. For reasons known only to Huberta herself, one day she decided to leave the lagoon adjacent to the Tugela River where she had been living all her life, and began walking south.

The first accounts of what would later become Huberta's famous trek appeared in newspapers a few days later. They recounted the story told by a group of sugar estate workers who had discovered a hippo casually munching sugar cane on the estate where they worked. The tale caught the public's imagination and within days Hubert the Hippo, as this unusual migrant had become known, was front-page news. It was only much, much later that everyone would realise that Hubert was, in fact, Huberta!

The public and paparazzi

By January 1929, Huberta had travelled as far south as Tongaat. That was when she took up residence in the nearby Umhlanga lagoon after being rudely disturbed by a passing motorist while resting on a bridge one night.

The locals, excited by the presence of a real-life celebrity in their midst, regarded her as a tourist attraction. Tour operators organised bus trips to see her and a flood of visitors brought her food. Huberta had indeed become big news.

Right Huberta the wandering hippo first made her rather startling appearance in Durban, before making her way south in one of the most incredible animal journeys ever recorded in South African history.

Did you know?

Between 1928 and 1931, a wild hippo the public came to know as Huberta became world famous when she walked the 1600 kilometres from KwaZulu-Natal to East London in the Eastern Cape.

A month later, she was on the move again. Her giant footprints were spotted on the greens of the Beechwood golf course and then, a few days later, some hippo tracks were found on a nearby housing estate. The locals maintained that she had been looking for a house in the district, but couldn't find one with a large enough bathroom!

After a brief sojourn in Pinetown reservoir, Huberta's next stop was Durban Country Club, where she turned up at the front gate late on the evening of 31 March. Needless to say, the appearance of a wandering hippo caused not a little commotion as all the rather fashionable guests rushed out of building to gawp at her. Apparently uncomfortable with all the attention she was garnering, she fled across the golf course, breaking down one or two fences in her haste to get away.

During the early hours of the following morning, 1 April, Huberta made her first full-blown public appearance by entering Durban itself, this time making a bee-line for West Street, where a policeman discovered her loitering outside West Street Pharmacy. As dawn brought more and more onlookers, she ambled away in the direction of the Federal Hotel. After that, she strolled through Victoria Park and finally into the quiet and cool waters of the Umgeni River mouth.

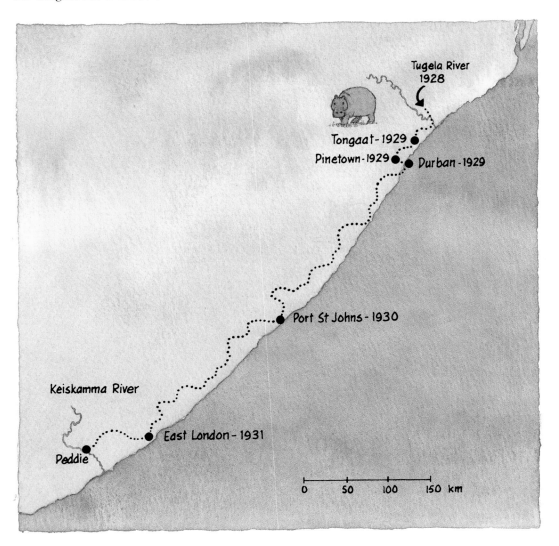

Left Huberta's astounding migration from the Tugela River, through Tongaat, Pinetown, Durban, Port St Johns, East London and, finally, to Peddie on the Keiskamma River took three years to complete and covered over 1600 kilometres.

The press were hot on her heels by this time and so were a number of the nation's zookeepers, particularly those from Johannesburg Zoo, where a lonely female hippo was pining away for want of companionship. (At the time, Huberta was still Hubert, remember.) Concerned that 'Hubert' was being harassed, the Natal Provincial Council ordered that he be left alone and proclaimed him 'royal game', which meant that he could not be captured or shot without a permit.

After leaving Durban, Huberta continued on her journey south. A local Indian community beat drums in her honour and declared her the 'Protector of the Poor'; there was talk among the Zulus that she was in some way connected to the revered spirit of Shaka, because she spent so much time in sacred Zulu pools; and the Pondo people suggested that she might be the reincarnation of a famous *sangoma*, which is why they left her unmolested – despite the fact that she would occasionally ravage their maize crops.

By March 1930, she had reached Port St Johns, where she took up residence in the Mzimvubu River. (The word *Mzimvubu* means 'home of the hippo', although at the time no hippo had been seen there in living memory.)

On the road again

Six months later, Huberta was on the move again, this time in the direction of the Wild Coast area. She would usually remain out of sight during the day and only leave the safety of the water at night in order to dine on the succulent plants that lined the river.

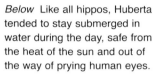

Below Like all hippos, Huberta tended to stay submerged in water during the day, safe from the heat of the sun and out of the way of prying human eyes.

By this time, her every move was being avidly followed by a worldwide audience, but not every local was happy at the thought of having a hippo in the area. Many farmers, for example, complained that her enormous appetite was ruining their crops, which is why Huberta was sometimes 'encouraged' to move on.

By March 1931, Huberta had reached East London, where – according to a local train driver, who had found her sleeping on the railway line – she had moved off into the bush, but only after he had repeatedly blown his whistle and finally, out of desperation, gently nudged her with his train. Just over a month later, the ever-wandering hippo reached the Keiskamma River near Peddie, which is where her luck finally ran out.

A farmer and his two sons found hippo tracks on their farm and followed them down to the river, where they spotted the hulking mammal wallowing in the water. Without thinking they immediately opened fire. They managed to wound Huberta, but didn't kill her, so they returned the next morning to finish the job.

A public outcry followed Huberta's untimely death, and although the three men pleaded ignorance about the hippo's identity, they were each fined £25 – a considerable sum at the time – for destroying Royal Game.

Experts from the Kaffrarian Museum (now known as the AmaThole Museum) in King William's Town later recovered Hubert the hippo from the river, realised that he was, in fact, a she, and put Huberta's body on display, where she still remains as a popular attraction today.

Ruler of Africa's waterways

Although the common river hippopotamus (*Hippopotamus amphibius*) is now largely confined to protected areas south of the Sahara, in ancient times, they were found throughout Europe, India, Madagascar and across Africa – murals depict Egyptian pharaohs hunting hippos in the Nile delta, which is probably why these animals are no longer found in Egypt.

Hippos usually spend their days in the water, protecting their thick but sensitive skin from sun damage, and their nights on land foraging for food. With an adult male weighing in at around three tons, and being the second-largest land animal after elephants, their environmental impact is significant. An adult hippo, for example, will consume approximately 40 kilograms of food at a sitting.

Generally gregarious and territorial, hippos tend to live in pods of 10–15 individuals, sometimes remaining on the same property for their full life span of 20–30 years, unless driven out by drought or overcrowding. Pods are usually made up of one adult male and a number of breeding females, plus their offspring. Non-breeding males are tolerated in the pod until they reach breeding age, after which they are forced out and join bachelor herds or live alone in marginal habitat.

Hippo cows first conceive between the ages of seven and nine years, and have a gestation period of eight months, with most hippo calves being born in shallow water or at the water's edge, usually during the rainy season. Hippo calves can swim before they can walk and are initially suckled underwater, with the mother lying on her side at the river or lagoon and the calf coming to the surface of the water to breathe about once every minute. (Adults can stay under water for a maximum of five minutes.)

Under normal circumstances, hippos are generally not aggressive toward humans, although they do become extremely dangerous if an intruder comes between them and the water, or between a mother and her calf.

The hippopotamus

Behold the hippopotamus!
We laugh at how he looks to us,
And yet in moments dank and grim,
I wonder how we look to him.
Peace, peace, thou hippopotamus!
We really look all right to us,
As you no doubt delight the eye
Of other hippopotami.
– Ogden Nash (1935)

Save the penguin!

In April 1968, the oil tanker *Esso Essen* began leaking oil after it struck a submerged object about five kilometres from the Cape Peninsula. About 15 000 tons of crude oil were spilled into the sea and swept towards the coast by strong winds and a higher-than-usual tide. The oil slick was to devastate some of the Cape's finest beaches, but that was nothing compared to the effect it had on any sea birds unfortunate enough to get in its way.

The *Esso Essen* oil spill was Cape Town's first taste of this particular kind of tragedy, but it was far from being its last. And, of the more than 3000 penguins affected by the oil spill, one particular individual stands out: an African penguin who came to be known as Gregory Peck.

The sweeping black tide

As the oil slick swept ashore, it brought with it literally hundreds of oil-covered penguins. This was a disaster of unprecedented proportions, and the Society for the Prevention of Cruelty to Animals (SPCA) was forced to mobilise a huge relief operation. The injured birds had to be captured, transported from the seashore where they had beached, cleaned and rehabilitated, and finally returned to the ocean. To make matters worse, very few people had any experience of this kind of rescue operation or knew how to rehabilitate birds affected by oil pollution.

As the number of sick and injured birds mounted, appeals went out over the radio for volunteers and a huge number of people came forward to help. However, it was also realised that, given the fact that an ever-increasing number of sea birds were being affected by coastal pollution – and oil pollution, in particular – a specific organisation needed to be established in order to address the problem, and to try to stem the decline in the numbers of a variety of southern African coastal birds. This resulted in the setting up of the South African National Foundation for the Conservation of Coast Birds (SANCCOB).

As part of SANCCOB's *Esso Essen* operation, a number of generous individuals offered their homes as rehabilitation centres for the affected penguins. These were places where, after the birds had been cleaned and treated, they could be fed and looked after until they regained enough strength to be returned to the wild.

One such couple was Ernst and Althea Westphal who lived in Newlands, Cape Town. Three months after the *Esso Essen* disaster, Professor and Mrs Westphal received yet another fairly anonymous penguin to join the garden full of birds they already had in their care. This bird, a juvenile by all appearances, had already been cleaned and treated, but wasn't strong enough to be returned to the ocean.

Below Besides being highly toxic, crude oil clogs up birds' feathers, rendering the penguin's natural waterproofing ineffective. With no protection from the cold water, birds may die of hypothermia.

Over the days that followed, the newcomer slowly began to regain some of his lost appetite and it wasn't long before he was gulping down his allotted number of pilchards each day. In fact, that alone was nothing to distinguish this particular individual from any of his contemporaries.

In due course, the young penguin was declared fit and ready for his return to the wild. The red plastic rings that had been attached to each of his flippers when he had first been brought in, were removed and replaced with a numbered metal ring issued by the Department of Fisheries. He was now officially bird number 640.

Shortly afterwards, penguin 640 and a group of other rehabilitated birds were taken to Bloubergstrand and released onto the beach. Without the slightest hesitation, they all waddled down to the water, dipped into the waves and vanished into the great blue yonder. Everyone assumed it was the end of yet another successful operation.

But then, as it would turn out, everyone was wrong…

Gregory returns

It was 10 days later that SANCCOB received a telephone call from a woman who owned a house fronting onto Blouberg beach. She had a penguin in her garage and didn't know what to do. She had noticed that the bird was tagged, which indicated it had been ashore before.

'Did you read its number?' someone asked.

'Yes, it's number 640,' she said.

This, however, was not a matter for rejoicing – released birds were supposed to stay released, and the workers at SANCCOB went out of their way to ensure that treated birds did not form any attachments with their human handlers, because when this happened it was sometimes impossible for them to be successfully rehabilitated for the wild.

Bird number 640 was thus brought in for tests, but he seemed perfectly healthy, so soon afterwards he was released into the ocean again.

A week later, SANCCOB received another telephone call, again from a Blouberg resident. The woman in question had gone for a walk on the beach and had been followed home by a penguin. He had a ring tag, too. His number was 640.

Penguin 640, who by this time was gaining something of a reputation for himself, was once more taken to the Westphals' house in Newlands where he was again weighed and tested. He was a perfectly healthy bird, so he was shipped out to Robben Island a couple of days later and released by the Department of Prisons.

No one is quite sure when Penguin 640 was first named Gregory Peck, but four days later Gregory was back on dry land again. This time he had walked out of the sea at Blouberg-strand and had been escorted across the beach by two poodles.

The poodles belonged to a Mrs Malan, who had returned home to find her dogs and the penguin sitting patiently in the garden. She had initially tried to shoo the bird away, but it just kept on coming back and seemed to want to go into the house. In the end, she relented and Gregory and his two minders made their way into the kitchen and settled themselves quite contentedly in front of the stove.

It was difficult to know what to do. Mrs Malan had offered her guest some fish from the refrigerator, but he had turned up his nose in disdain. Worried that he would be hungry and in need of special medical treatment, she had telephoned the local newspaper, which had recommended SANCCOB, which, in turn, had referred her to Mrs Westphal. However, the newspaper had also sent around a reporter to investigate this intriguing story and the next morning Penguin 640 had made the headlines.

Bird number 640 – Gregory Peck – was now an official celebrity.

Did you know?

The African (or jackass) penguin, a bird unique to southern Africa, is estimated to have had its numbers reduced by 90 per cent over the last 100 years.

Gregory gets a job

It was obvious that Gregory was not going to stay out at sea, at least not for the time being. But what to do with him, that was the question? The best option, it seemed, was to use him as a control bird. That is, one that is fairly used to its human handlers and could be used to help train new volunteers. And so this is what Gregory became. And he took to his new role like... well, like a duck to water. But it was evident that Gregory kept himself slightly aloof from the other birds. He would swim with them, show an interest in what was going on, but didn't really join in with the group. He was, however, very curious about his human companions, particularly when any newcomers visited.

And so Gregory slowly settled into his routine, showing no interest in returning to the wild. Newlands, it seems, was a suburb that suited a penguin.

Around November, a change became apparent in Gregory: he began to moult. His adolescent plumage, which had gradually turned more brown than black, began to turn a dull grey. Then his feathers became moth-eaten and unruly, and he started to eat more and gain weight. Gregory was growing up.

Top right Not only can the cleaning process be traumatic for wild birds, but it is also very labour intensive and penguins can deliver a nasty bite!

A happy ending

It took until after Christmas for Gregory to transform himself and, by January 1969, he was a lean, fully-grown penguin. That was when the Westphals received the greatest shock of all.

Awoken one night by the sound of what sounded like an entire flock of African penguins braying in the garden, they went outside to find two penguins performing what could only be described as a courtship dance. And Gregory was the one being courted. Gregory was not a he after all, but a she! Gregory was, in fact, Gregorina!

And when Gregorina's 'companion' was ready to be return to the wild, Gregorina went with him. They were released as a pair off Dassen Island and swam away together, never to be seen again.

And thus the story of Gregory – or, rather, Gregorina – Peck ended happily ever after...

Enter Percy...

While Gregorina Peck enjoyed the limelight and public attention in the late 1960s, some 30 years later another penguin stepped into the spotlight in much the same circumstances. On 23 June 2000, the bulk ore carrier MV *Treasure* went down near Melkbos on the Cape West Coast. The following day, the first oiled birds were spotted on Robben Island, and three days after that, oil spilt from the vessel was threatening Dassen Island, home to more than 55 000 African penguins.

The African penguin

The African penguin (*Spheniscus demersus*) – also known as the jackass penguin because of its jackass-like bray – is one of about 20 species of penguin found throughout the world, but is the only one indigenous to the southern African coast.

This species, which is currently defined at 'vulnerable' in the Red Data Book, appears to have suffered a rapid decline in numbers over the last 100 years. In the 1930s, for example, it was estimated that there were at least 500 000 African penguins living on Dassen Island alone, but the entire species now numbers around 100 000 animals in total, and are distributed among three major breeding sites:

- Dassen Island, off Yzerfontein (approximately 30 000 birds)
- Dyer Island, near Gansbaai, (approximately 20 000 birds)
- St Croix Island, near Port Elizabeth (approximately 50 000 birds)

The causes of this drastic decline in numbers are thought to be:
- The massive disturbance of breeding sites in the 19th century due to guano mining.
- The harvesting of eggs for human consumption.
- A reduction in the penguin's natural food store as a result of over-fishing.
- The effects of coastal pollution, especially oil pollution.

Fortunately, Western Cape Nature Conservation had made provision for just such an eventuality after the sinking of the *Apollo Sea* in 1994.

At first the plan was merely to save those birds that had been affected by the oil by whisking them off to the SANCCOB rehabilitation centre in the suburb of Salt River in Cape Town, where they could be cleaned and treated before eventually being returned to the wild. However, on 2 July, when the full magnitude of the disaster had become apparent, the unprecedented decision was made to remove all the penguins from Dassen Island and then transport them to the Eastern Cape, where they would be released back into the ocean. It was estimated that by the time the birds had made their way back to Dassen Island, the pollution threat would be over.

Within a matter of days, a team of conservationists and their helpers descended on the island and then captured over 19 000 uncontaminated birds. From there, these birds were airlifted to Yzerfontein harbour, where they were repacked for their journey to Port Elizabeth. Some of the penguins were also fitted with transmitters so that their progress along the coast could be monitored. Most notable of these were Percy and his 'cousin' Pamela.

While Pamela dawdled off the coast of Port Elizabeth, gorging herself on the local fare, Percy – much to the wonder and amazement of an adoring public – headed straight back to Dassen Island. Within a week, he was in familiar waters and on the evening of 27 July, waddled back up onto the beach, having swept like a torpedo through 800 kilometres of shark-infested waters along the country's east coast. For his own safety, he was once again rather unceremoniously removed from the island to a place of safety, becoming in the process – for a few days at least – South Africa's most popular and most photographed 'celebrity'.

A few days later, Pamela was also monitored in the Dassen Island area, but she appears to have showed better sense than Percy and remained off-shore, away from the uncompromising glare of the public spotlight – women's intuition, perhaps.

This story, too, has a happy ending. In a follow-up report a year later, Dieter Oschadleus of the University of Cape Town's Avian Demography Unit, stated, 'After the traumatic experiences of being oiled, captured, transported, force-fed, medicated and living in a totally unnatural environment, the penguins have made a successful transition back into the wild.'[1]

Surprisingly, in spite of what could have been a disastrous episode, the breeding colony on Dassen Island showed a remarkable 25 per cent increase in population over the previous year.

Cleaning up

Crude oil is highly toxic if ingested and also clogs up the feathers of the bird. The feathers of sea birds such as penguins have a unique interlocking action. The feathers are barbed and 'lock' together to provide a waterproof seal that prevents water reaching the animal's skin. Oil clogs up the feathers, making the waterproofing ineffective. The bird thus becomes waterlogged and the cold water, from which the bird is usually well insulated, causes hypothermia.

Cleaning birds affected by oil pollution is not a simple task since care must be taken to protect the natural oiliness of the bird's feathers. In 1968, the most effective method was to use Fuller's Earth, a finely powdered clay that absorbs the oil on the bird's body. Over a period of days, the bird is sprinkled with this substance, which gently absorbs the oil, and is left on for about an hour after which it is gently washed off. Rubbing the bird's feathers is to be avoided since this is likely to both damage them and affect the natural water-repellent process.

Penguins also only eat 'live' food and, for this reason, they have to be force-fed a diet of pilchards while in captivity. This process involves gripping the bird firmly between the knees while forcing a dead fish head first into its gullet – a far from simple task, given the fact that the birds have extremely sharp beaks!

Nowadays, the birds are first rehydrated using a mixture of glucose and electrolytes – by inserting a tube into the bird's stomach – and are then cleaned. The birds are also given a medicinal dose of activated charcoal, which absorbs any oil the bird has ingested. Birds that are identified as being too weak for washing are put in an intensive-care unit and are force-fed pilchards to build their strength.

The washing process involves coating the birds with BD1 solution – the invention of a South African high-school student – which consists of recycled cooking oil and has been proved to be highly effective in breaking down the denser bunker oil.

The birds then go through a series of washes using progressively cleaner warm water baths and washing-up liquid. After the oil has been removed, the birds are rinsed.

They are fed throughout the process and are then moved to overnight drying rooms where they are placed under infra-red lamps. After this, they are 'swam' in special swimming tanks and given daily treatments of vitamins before being returned to the ocean.[2]

The mighty megamouth

The megamouth shark – so called because of its large, gaping snout – was not known to exist until the first specimen was caught off Kaneohe, Hawaii, on 15 November 1976. The animal in question had been swimming at a depth of about 165 metres and had become entangled in the sea anchor of an experimental trawler belonging to the United States Naval Undersea Centre.

The second specimen was caught in a gill net eight years later off the coast of California. In 1988, the third known specimen was found stranded on a beach at Mandurah, Western Australia, where it was initially mistaken for a whale. The fourth and fifth specimens were caught off the coast of Japan.

The sixth megamouth was caught alive and tagged before being returned to the ocean, where its behaviour was monitored for over 50 hours. That animal was found to be a vertical migrator, spending the day at a depth of around 150 metres and ascending to about 10–12 metres to feed during the night.

Hardly a dozen more of these little-known creatures have been seen since then, though they have now been spotted off the coasts of the Philippines, Senegal in West Africa, Indonesia and, more recently, southern Africa.

Facts and figures...

The megamouth shark (*Megachasma pelagios*), which has been described as looking like an enormous tadpole, is a large, slow-swimming, filter-feeding shark that uses its large mouth to scoop up tiny organisms – most notably krill and zooplankton – as it passes through the water. Its colour varies from grey to bluish-black above and pale grey below, while the tips of most of its fins are white. The inside of its huge mouth contains around 50 rows of numerous tiny teeth, though it is not considered dangerous to human swimmers.

Although the specimen found at Nature's Valley measured 3,5 metres and weighed 300 kilograms, a megamouth can grow to about five metres in length and weigh up to 500 kilograms.

Right The megamouth shark that washed up at Plettenberg Bay's Nature's Valley in 2002 is very rare indeed, and there have been fewer than a dozen recorded sightings of this reclusive animal.

Did you know?

An intact specimen of the extremely rare megamouth shark was washed up on the beach at Nature's Valley near Plettenberg Bay on 20 April 2002.

Little, however, is known about its habits and feeding behaviour, but it is thought to spend most of its time at depths of between 150 and 1000 metres.

The megamouth shark has no known natural predators, but has been observed on one occasion being attacked by a pod of sperm whales, which are predominantly squid eaters. Whether this was an isolated occurrence caused by competition for food is uncertain.

The megamouth is nevertheless probably the most primitive living species within the order Lamniformes, which includes the mako, white and porbeagle sharks, and probably evolved its filter-feeding independently from its 'cousin', the basking shark.

According to Dr Vic Cockcroft of the Centre for Dolphin Studies, 'We are very excited [about the Nature's Valley megamouth shark] because it is only the third female to be discovered to date and we know almost nothing about its biology, so we are keen to dissect and study it… They are rarely seen because they are usually far offshore feeding on plankton. We are unsure about their numbers. We have no information on how many there are.'[3]

Did you know?

South Africa, and its coastal waters, is home to some of the world's top record-breaking[4] animal species:
- The largest land mammal – the African Elephant.
- The smallest mammal – the dwarf shrew.
- The tallest animal – the giraffe.
- The fastest land mammal – the cheetah.
- The largest antelope – the eland.
- The largest bird – the ostrich.
- The heaviest flying bird – the kori bustard.

A fin breaks the surface…

Sharks are a much-maligned species and tend to get bad press, thanks in part to the popular media. The truth is sharks are at much greater risk from humans than humans are from sharks. Research suggests that shark numbers are declining and that certain species may well be endangered. The threats to shark numbers are all of human origin. They include:

- The use of gill nets by fishermen
- The shark-fin trade
- Indiscriminate fishing practices
- Pollution
- The use of shark nets.

According to statistics provided by the Natal Sharks Board, shark attacks on humans average about seven per year along the 2000 kilometres of coastline from the Mozambique border to Cape Town, and between 1990 and 2000 there was a total of only seven fatal shark attacks in South African waters.

An individual unfortunate enough to be attacked by a shark stands about a one-in-three chance of suffering serious injury and about a one-in-ten chance of being killed. In other words, even in the unlikely situation where one is attacked by a shark, there is a 70% chance that you will emerge from the encounter relatively unscathed.

Shark attacks on humans occur less frequently on beaches where shark nets are in place, but some animals inevitably become trapped in these nets and drown. Efforts are currently being made to reduce the number of shark nets and, where possible, replace them with other types of deterrent. For further information visit *www.shark.co.za*

Endnotes

1. 'Oiled penguins now readjusted', *Cape Argus*, 21 June 2002.
2. Marie Philip, *Gregory Jackass Penguin* (1971), Cape Town: David Philip Publishers.
3. Discovery Channel website: http://dsc.discovery.com/news

The Spirit World

The term 'ghost', at least in its archaic form, usually refers to a disembodied or distraught 'soul' that exists in the nether region that lies between our world – the world of the living – and the world of the dead. Many religions believe that prayer or meditation will facilitate the transition, or 'crossing over', for these troubled entities into heaven (Nirvana, Valhalla or Paradise) or hell (Hades, Purgatory or The Inferno). Ghosts or spirits should not, however, be confused with demons, which are usually defined as evil forces.

Some ghosts don't even know they're dead! It's only when they become aware of themselves that they disappear. Other ghosts manifest themselves after their earthly self has suffered a sudden and unexpected death. These ghosts usually have 'unfinished business' to complete, but there also so-called crisis ghosts, anniversary ghosts, replay ghosts, interactive ghosts, poltergeists, doppelgängers (ghosts of the living) – and a host of haunted paraphernalia, including houses, cars, and ordinary household appliances. And South Africans have, over time, experienced all of these ghostly interventions.

A poet, a prince and a pregnancy

My soul looked down from a vague height, with Death,
As unremembering how I rose or why,
And saw a sad land, weak with sweats of death
                                    – Wilfred Owen: The Show (1918)

One of South Africa's most famous crisis-ghost appearances involves the World War I poet, Wilfred Owen, who appeared to his brother, Harold, on 11 November 1918. Later, Harold would describe an incident in which he saw his brother's ghost in his three-volume auto-biographical memoir, *Journey from Obscurity (1960–1965)*.

At the time of his death, Wilfred Owen was fighting with the 5th Manchester Regiment of the British Army on the Western Front in Europe. His brother, Harold, was serving on the British cruiser HMS *Astraea*, which was anchored in Table Bay, Cape Town. The *Astraea* had recently arrived from the Cameroons and Harold, who had been feeling depressed and 'flat', as he described it, for a week, was in his cabin when his brother materialised. Wilfred suddenly appeared sitting in Harold's chair, wearing a khaki uniform and with blood streaming down his face. Though Harold knew it was impossible for his brother to be there, he spoke to him nonetheless.

'Wilfred, how did you get here?' he asked.

Wilfred, he claimed, looked at him in some distress, but didn't answer. He then broke into a broad smile and vanished a moment later.

Although Harold reasoned that seeing his brother at that moment may well have been a figment of his imagination, he knew with absolute certainty that Wilfred was dead. It would later be established that poet Wilfred Owen had been killed in action at the Sambre Canal in France, on 4 November, one week earlier. Harold realised, then, that he had felt depressed and anxious about his brother from the time of his death.

Prince Christian Victor at the Cape

Another famous crisis ghost, though one of a different nature, was that of Prince Christian Victor Anton von Schleswig-Holstein, grandson of Queen Victoria and first cousin to the German Emperor, Kaiser Wilhelm I. The difference between the ghost of Prince Christian Victor and that of Wilfred Owen is that, in the case of the prince, the ghost appeared over a year after he had died, at a time when his sister, Princess Marie Louise, was in distress.

Prince Christian Victor was born on 14 April 1867 and later embarked on a military career, eventually landing at the Cape for a third tour of duty in Africa at the start of the South African (Anglo-Boer) War in October 1899. Some two years later, in 1901, the prince was appointed aide-de-camp to General Roberts, but shortly afterwards, he was struck down by enteric fever while in Pretoria and died on 20 October of the same year. In accordance with his wishes that he be laid to rest among his comrades, Prince Christian Victor was buried in Pretoria in the military section of the old Pretoria cemetery.

A princess in pain

Princess Marie Louise had originally met her husband, Prince Aribert of Anhalt Dessau, fourth son of Duke Leopold of Anhalt, in 1889. They had married on 6 July 1891 at Windsor Castle, but things went badly from the outset. Marie Louise found that her life was ruled by the strict etiquette insisted upon by her husband. What would also be revealed was that Prince Aribert considered the marriage purely one of convenience and it was soon clear to Marie Louise that her husband had no interest in her: they only met at meals and would sometimes not see each other for days on end.

In 1900, after nine years of marriage, the princess decided she had to get away at least temporarily, so she went, without her husband's permission, on a trip to United States and Canada. It was this action that was to prove decisive. First, she received a telegram from her father-in-law, ordering her to return immediately to Anhalt, then a second telegram arrived an hour later, from Queen Victoria, which stated: 'Tell my granddaughter to come home to me. VR.'

The reason for such apparent urgency only became apparent later when Princess Marie Louise returned home to Windsor. In her absence, Prince Aribert had accused her of deserting her marital duties, and was

Below Killed on foreign soil and far from his homeland, Prince Christian Victor is buried in the military section of the old Pretoria cemetery.

demanding that their marriage be annulled. Her father-in-law, the supreme law in Anhalt, acceded to this demand and declared the marriage null and void, using the justification that Marie Louise had not given his son any children, proof of invalidity in Anhalt. For the rest of her life, however, Marie Louise would consider herself a married woman, and it was only afterwards that she would learn that the real reason for the annulment was that her husband had been caught in a compromising situation with another man.

The prince reappears

It was shortly after these traumatic events that Princess Marie Louise, who was living in London at the time, encountered the ghost of her brother, who had died in Pretoria some 18 months previously. According to her own account, the door of the upstairs room in which she was sitting alone opened, and in walked her elder brother, Christian Victor.

'Oh, Kicky,' – the prince's pet name – she said, 'How nice to see you again.'

Her brother first said that he had come to see that she was 'all right and happy', then he sat down in the chair next to the fire and the two of them talked for a short while. Eventually, he got up, repeated that he was very happy and that all was well with him; then he told her not to follow him downstairs, and walked out of the room.

After he had gone, she realised that he had been dressed in khaki, and had not been wearing his usual ribbons. Then she remembered that during the South African (Anglo-Boer) War an order had been issued that officers were not to wear their ribbons, so that the enemy would not be able to distinguish them from their men. It was only at this point, she claimed, that she realised that the dearly loved brother with whom she had been speaking had died 18 months previously, and lay in his resting place in South Africa.

Later, on the same afternoon, Princess Marie Louise described the incident to her sister, who, at the time, was sitting in the same chair her brother had occupied.

'I know he has been here. I feel it…' her sister replied.

Princess Marie Louise published her memoirs, *My Memories of Six Reigns*, in 1956.

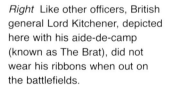

Right Like other officers, British general Lord Kitchener, depicted here with his aide-de-camp (known as The Brat), did not wear his ribbons when out on the battlefields.

Did you know?

It has been suggested that so-called 'cold spots', which are often said to precede the appearance of ghostly figures, are due to the fact that when these ghosts materialise, they draw heat from the room, which they use as energy in order to give themselves 'substance'.

A cottage in Zulu Africa...

One of South Africa's most famous replay ghosts – those who return again and again to the same spot to 'relive' a specific event – originates in the Eastern Cape. This apparition was first reported in 1952, but the case gained a wider audience after it was described as 'one of the strangest accounts I have ever come across', by psychical researcher and author, Andrew MacKenzie. John and Anne Spencer also document the story in their book *The Encyclopedia of Ghosts and Spirits*.

According to this latter account, the story of this '...haunting of a cottage in Zulu Africa',[1] was first related by Margaret Leigh, an occupational therapist working at a mission hospital in what was then Transkei. Her husband, who was a doctor on contract from England, was involved in research work at the same hospital. The Leighs lived in a small stone cottage, 'which had a thatched circular living room with a small built-in cupboard on the thick rough-hewn stone wall'.[2]

The first time the ghost made its presence felt was when Margaret was playing with her cat, Tivy. There was a knock on the door and the cat leapt away in fright, but when Margaret got up to see who was outside, there was no one there. This, it seems, was merely the first of many such visitations. In fact, the knocking began to occur with such frequency that the Leighs stopped answering the door – much to the consternation of their legitimate guests.

Eventually, the ghost began entering the house and, on each occasion, they would hear it shuffle from the door across the floor to the couch. Then it would sit down for a short while, after which it would get up and shuffle to the cupboard in the wall and then return to the couch.

The Leighs eventually learnt that their ghostly visitor was someone the locals usually referred to as 'Cousin John', and that he was the dead cousin of a man who had once lived in the house. But what they also discovered was that Cousin John had been something of a drinker and that he had kept his booze in the cupboard in the house to hide it from his wife. Apparently, he kept his better half away from his hidey-hole by telling her that there was a dangerous bees' nest inside!

Cousin John and his wife had been childless and when Margaret Leigh discovered that she was pregnant, the visits increased markedly, only stopping after the birth of the child. But there is a fascinating addendum to this story. At the end of the Leighs' contract in the Transkei, they returned to the United Kingdom, but made a return visit to the area three years later. They learnt that the new occupants of the house were also experiencing Cousin John's ghostly presence.

'Your wife's pregnant, isn't she?' asked Margaret.

'No, she isn't,' the man replied – but it turned out that she was indeed pregnant and gave birth nine months later.

Ghost Country

The Spokeveld ('Ghost Country') – marked as such on some old maps of the region – is the stretch of veld between Ceres and Beaufort West in the Western Cape and it is here that the famed phantom wagon appears to the unsuspecting. According to legend, the wagon has a devilish driver and appears in the small hours of the morning, careering helter-skelter across the landscape in order to 'attack' innocent travellers as they move through the district.

Although the existence of this ghost appears to have been an accepted fact among the locals during the 18th and 19th centuries – hence the name 'spokeveld' – arguably, its most famous sighting occurred towards the end of the 19th century and was reported by Major

Alfred Ellis of the West India Regiment. Major Ellis, who spent some time in South Africa, recorded his sighting in his book, *South African Sketches*, published in London in 1887.

The story recounted by Major Ellis was told to him by a man named Lutterodt. According to Lutterodt, the incident occurred in the month of November when he and three companions – a passenger named Serrurier from Conrader's Fontein, a visitor from Cape Town and Anthony de Heer – were travelling from Ceres to Beaufort West.[3]

En route, however, they encountered a problem with one of the wheels on the wagon on which they were travelling and this delayed them considerably. It took most of the night to fix the problem, and they only set off again at about 3 am. It was not long after they had resumed their journey that the horses stopped suddenly and appeared to be in a state of agitation. Although the driver managed to coax the horses, it wasn't long before they stopped again.

It was then that everyone on board heard the sound of another wagon approaching at great speed: they could hear the driver shouting as he cracked his whip, the rumble of wheels and the sound of pounding hooves. Then they saw the wagon itself. According to Lutterodt, it had a white canvas canopy, was being pulled by 14 mules and was heading straight for them. To save themselves, Lutterodt and his companions leapt to the ground and fled to the side of the road, but De Heer – the driver – tried to swing his vehicle out of the way.

At the last moment, he shouted: 'Where do you think you're going?'

Below The ghostly wagon would appear without warning and then attempt to drive other travellers from the road.

'To hell!' replied the other driver.

A moment later, the ghostly driver swerved to the side, careered past the stalled wagon – and promptly vanished into thin air!

Lutterodt maintained that the only way to save oneself when confronted by the phantom wagon was to challenge the phantom driver, which is exactly what De Heer had done. There is a price to pay, however: the person who makes the challenge is doomed to die shortly afterwards. De Heer's body, or so Lutterodt maintained, was discovered a week later, amid the shattered remnants of his wagon and horses, at the bottom of a ravine at Hottentot's Kloof.

On the road again...

Although there is a surprising number of early recorded ghost sightings on South Africa's dry and dusty roads, the most oft-repeated – and certainly one of the most chilling – is the story of the so-called Uniondale Hitchhiker, who is thought to be the ghost of 22-year-old Maria Charlotte Roux, who was killed in a motor car accident in the early hours of the morning of 12 April 1968. Miss Roux was killed when the car in which she was travelling with her fiancé veered off the road. Her ghost was first reported 10 years later, when she appeared to South African army corporal Dawie van Jaarsveld, who was travelling by motorcycle along the Barrandas-Willowmore road, en route to visit his girlfriend.

Van Jaarsveld stopped to offer a lift to an attractive brunette wearing a blue top and dark trousers who was hitchhiking at the side of the road. He gave her the spare helmet he was carrying with him, and an earplug so that she could listen to the radio as they travelled. About 20 minutes later, Van Jaarsveld skidded after he felt an imbalance on the weight of his motorcycle. He managed to retain control of the vehicle but when he looked back, his passenger had vanished and his spare helmet was once again strapped to the rear seat.

According to an account of a subsequent investigation into this incident, reported in *The Encyclopedia of Ghosts and Spirits*[4], an investigator by the name of David Barritt, later visited Van Jaarsveld with a photograph of Maria Charlotte Roux – and Dawie van Jaarsveld positively identified Miss Roux as the person to whom he given a lift on the night in question.

The same young woman appeared to Anton Le Grange in May 1976, who also stopped to offer her a lift in his car. In this instance, however, the phantom hitchhiker, who was sitting in the back seat Le Grange's car, gave a terrifying scream and vanished without warning. What makes the Le Grange account all the more significant is the fact that a police officer, Constable Potgieter, happened to be following Le Grange's car when the incident occurred and claims to have witnessed the rear door open and close, as if someone was climbing in or out of the vehicle.

An experience similar to that described by Van Jaarsveld also allegedly occurred to a man named Ken Dodds in 1980. In this instance, Dodds described feeling the 'presence' of another person on his motorcycle shortly after he had passed a young woman standing at the side of the road. He claimed to have felt the pressure of arms around his waist and was struck repeatedly on his helmet. When he stopped to investigate, there was no one behind him.

The most recent reported appearance of the ghost occurred in May 1987. A young woman matching the ghost's description – though this time dressed in white – was seen at around 9.30 pm in the evening by the Van Jaarsveld family (no relation) while they were driving from Oudtshoorn to Port Elizabeth. Mr and Mrs Van Jaarsveld and their 14-year-old daughter, Marietha, all saw the same woman in white standing at the side of the road with one leg slightly raised as if about to climb onto an invisible motorcycle. Marietha claimed that, at the same moment she saw the hitchhiker, she felt a chill envelope her, and the family felt a 'ghostly presence' in the car for the next 20 kilometres, after which it dissipated...

Haunted houses

It seems almost inevitable that old houses, especially those long abandoned or falling into disrepair, eventually become 'haunted'. Those that appear to be the genuine article, however, are much less common.

The ghost of Erasmus Castle

One of Gauteng's most famous 'haunted' houses is the so-called Erasmus Castle, overlooking the Delmas road, east of Pretoria. This building, which was built by an eccentric farmer named Jochemus Johannes Petrus Erasmus in 1903, had its 'haunted' reputation enhanced after it was featured in a 1946 Afrikaans ghost movie called *Hier's Ons Weer* ('Here We Are Again').

The farm on which Erasmus Castle is located came into the Erasmus family in about 1888, when – according to at least one version of the story – Carel Erasmus, Jochemus Erasmus's father, obtained 27 000 morgen of land in exchange for 'a pair of velvet trousers and a salted horse'.[5]

Not long afterwards, Jochemus built a house on the property, but Carel didn't like it and ordered his son to build a 'decent' house, one that was 'worthy of the family'.[6] The result of this edict was the house that we know today, which was built at a cost of £6,800, plus £400 for 'extras' – a small fortune at the time.

Below The grand old Erasmus Castle is today the headquarters of Armscor and has been restored to its former glory.

In time, 'Erasmus Castle', as the house came to be know, became a local landmark and was frequently marked on maps of the district. Rumours also sprang up that the house was haunted – but not with just a single ghost, with two or three! These ghosts, or so it is alleged, are the spirits of two or three of Jochemus's children, who were kept locked up in the main tower after it was found they were suffering from leprosy. It is the ghosts of these poor infants, some argue, that still roam the castle today.

In 1976, a day after Jochemus Erasmus's eldest daughter died at the age of 91 years, the Transvaal Provincial Administration expropriated the property in order to build a large academic hospital on the site. The hospital was, however, never built and over the decade or so that followed, the building fell into disrepair until it was acquired and restored by Armscor, its present owners, in the early 1990s.

In his book, *Ghosts of Pretoria*,[7] Eric Bolsmann tells an amusing story that has added to the house's 'haunted' reputation. The incident in question occurred after the Erasmus family had vacated the property and before Armscor had taken ownership.

One particular night, a veld fire threatened the property and necessitated calling out the fire brigade. However, what the firemen didn't know was that a night watchman used to sleep on the stoep and that the man was hard of hearing and wore a long, old-fashioned white nightshirt. When the fire brigade arrived at the scene of the fire, the night watchman, disturbed suddenly from his sleep, leapt up off his bed and ran around in panic on the veranda. As Eric Bolsmann says, that indeed must have been a 'ghostly' sight to remember!

Over the last 10 years or so, there have been numerous 'sightings' and 'incidents' involving ghostly apparitions at the grand old house. One of the most recent occurred in 1992 during an official Armscor function, when one guest claimed to have seen a woman who appeared to have just stepped out of the 19th century.

What's hiding at Hiddingh?

Hiddingh House, on Newlands Avenue in the Cape Town suburb of the same name, was built during the early 19th century, probably as a residence for cavalry officers serving Lord Charles Somerset, but by the beginning of the 20th century the property, which was then located in the middle of a forest and was without electricity, was already referred to by the locals as a 'haunted house'.

In 1910, the house was acquired by the Boonzaier family, but Gregoire Boonzaier – interviewed by Margaret Williamson for her 1993 book *Haunted Corners* – vehemently denied the presence of a ghost at Hiddingh House. According to the then elderly Mr Boonzaier – he was 83 at the time of the interview – the house was old and somewhat creaky, but it was definitely not haunted. The sounds some locals liked to ascribe to ghostly visitations were caused, he maintained, by either the wind as it whistled through the trees around the property, or simply the usual – and quite explicable – sounds made by the old house itself.

With regards the stories of ghostly appearances, particularly that of a woman in a white dress who appeared outside the door to the drawing room and then vanished, he had an even more prosaic explanation... His father, Gregoire explained, was something of an eccentric who insisted that neither wife nor children should be seen or heard when he was entertaining visitors. On such occasions, Boonzaier Senior would retire to the drawing room and mother and children would be instructed to remain out of sight. Mrs Boonzaier's only appearance would be when she delivered her husband's tea. When this was required, she would go only as far as the door, where she would hand over the tea tray without showing herself. It was simply their 'domestic peculiarities', Gregoire argued, that created the fiction of a ghost, and nothing more. The Boonzaiers moved out of the house around 1920 and during the following 20 years the house stood empty for long periods. It was during this period in particular that the house's 'haunted' reputation took seed and grew.

The next family to move in for any length of time were the Spears.[8] According to a letter Frank Spears, the owner, wrote to Margaret Williamson, their maid, Mary Basson, claimed to have seen a number of ghosts, including a 'little lady' who would open the

Top left The somewhat spooky Hiddingh House may originally been built as a residence for Lord Charles Somerset's cavalry officers.

drawing room door and walk in, on a number of occasions. These appearances always occurred during broad daylight and, amazingly, never frightened Mary because, so she claimed, the ghosts 'seemed like nice people'!

Mrs Spears also claimed to have seen the figure of a ghostly woman at the end of the bed one night. On this occasion, the ghost walked around to her husband's side of the bed, where it seemed to study the books on the bedside table before vanishing. At that point, Mr Spears woke up. He had just dreamt, so he told his wife, that a woman had come into the room, bent over and kissed him on the cheek.

'Unfortunately,' he added wistfully, 'she never came again, or if she did, I didn't wake up and enjoy it!'[9]

After the Spears came the Siddons family, who were aware of the house's reputation but weren't at all scared by it – despite the fact that they claimed to have heard on a number of occasions, a loud crash from the bathroom, only to find nothing was disturbed or broken when they went to investigate. There were also occasions when the lights would come on at night for no apparent reason, always between midnight and 3 am.

More recent owners of the property have also reported strange happenings at the house, often involving the sighting of a young woman wearing an old-fashioned white dress, but who this 'person' might be remains a mystery. One suggested explanation is that she is the ghost of a young woman who, many years ago – when cavalry officers occupied the house – fell down the stairs during a party and broke her neck.

The ghost of John Murray

Zwartkoppies Hall, situated just outside Pretoria, was proclaimed a museum in 1986 following an agreement between the Sammy Marks Trust Estate and the National Cultural and Open-Air Museum in Pretoria. Since then, the house and its grounds have been painstakingly restored to their former glory.

Sammy Marks was a Russian Jew born in Neustadt, Lithuania, on 11 July 1844, and although he arrived, penniless, in South Africa at the age of 24, he was to make his fortune on the diamond fields of Kimberley, in the process becoming one of the country's most successful industrialists and mining magnates.

In 1882, Marks moved to the Transvaal and purchased land adjacent to the farm Zwartkoppies, and it was on this newly acquired property that he built Zwartkoppies Hall. It was here, then, that he and his wife, Bertha, took up residence, raising their family.

It was sometime in the early 1880s that John Murray arrived on the scene. Little or nothing is known about him other than that he was a well-educated, though penniless Scot who once acted as a transport driver for Sammy Marks, transporting heavy pieces of machinery from Durban to Eerste Fabrieken. Marks, however, took a liking to Murray, brought him back to the house one afternoon,

The Society for Psychical Research

The Society for Psychical Research was founded in Cambridge, England, in 1882, primarily to investigate five categories of interest. They were: telepathy, hypnotism, 'sensitives' (mediums), apparitions and 'the various physical phenomena commonly called Spiritualistic'. From the outset, the organisation was composed of a number of physicists, physiologists, astronomers, zoologists and a wide range of eminent scientists from various professions and, in so far as it can be described as having a 'corporate identity', was essentially sceptical and rigorously scientific by nature.

One of the first investigations carried out by the society was to conduct a census to determine the percentage of people who had experienced a ghostly or hallucinatory event. To this end, they carried out a survey in which they asked 17,000 people to answer the following question: 'Have you ever, when believing yourself to be completely awake, had a vivid impression of seeing or being touched by a living being or inanimate object, or of hearing a voice, which impression, so far as you could discover, was not due to any external cause?'[10]

Of those 1684 participants who responded in the affirmative, 1029 were women and 655 were men. In other words, 9,9 per cent of the recipients had experienced a supernatural event. In some respects, this figure of 10% is still generally considered to represent the percentage of people in the general population who have experienced a paranormal occurrence.

Despite the fact that the Society has come in for its fair share of criticism over the years – mainly over the controversial nature of its subject matter – it is well to remember that it is able to boast at least 11 Nobel Prize winners among its members over the past 100 years.

and finding the conversation interesting, asked him to stay the night. And Murray never left. The unlikely duo of Marks the industrialist and Murray the penniless transport driver became firm friends. Later on, Murray worked as a bookkeeper and a kind of general companion to Marks, but spent most of his time reading to Marks and bringing to his attention texts and matters he thought would be of interest to him.

John Murray died at Zwartkoppies in 1905, and stories that a ghost inhabited the house began to circulate in the 1980s, shortly after the restoration of the Zwartkoppies property began. Labourers working on the site refused to enter the house after dark, fearing that the building was inhabited by a 'presence', while a waitress working in the tea garden even claimed that the ghost pinched her bottom one afternoon while she was walking along a corridor that leads from the tea garden to the kitchen.

A museum guide, Agnes Kruger, also reported encountering a ghost on a number of occasions while working at the museum. She also claimed that these appearances were but one of many 'strange happenings'[11] that occurred on the premises.

'The doors to the rooms in the house are always left open, but for reasons unknown to me, on some days, the door to John Murray's room is closed. When we first noticed this, we felt odd. Not one of the employees had reason to close the door. Shortly after being opened, it was mysteriously closed again. When we entered the room, it felt ice cold. We experienced the same phenomenon over and over until we came to the conclusion that John Murray has certain days when he wants to be left alone. Today, all employees of the museum respect his wishes. If the door to his room is closed, we leave it closed for the day.'[12]

There is also the story of the English visitor on a tour of the house who asked whether a baby had died in one of the rooms. The child to whom she was inadvertently referring was Leonora Josephine, who was four months old when she died in 1890. On entering John Murray's room, the same woman asked who the dark man with the deep-set eyes was, who was standing at the foot of the bed. A Japanese guest also bowed in the dining room to 'pay her respects' to the spirit presence she sensed there.

Intrigued by these stories, Pretoria writer, Eric Bolsmann, decided to conduct an experiment and have someone stay in the house over night. He obtained permission from the museum authorities and eventually arranged for Peter van Raay, the general manager of the hotel Villa Via and his assistant, Shaun Strydom, to stay in John Murray's room on the night of Friday, 13 December 1996.

On the night in question, he dropped them off after dark and picked them up at 7.30 the following morning. And, did they meet the ghost of John Murray? Unfortunately not. The two men stayed awake talking until 2 am, then fell asleep and slept like babies.[13]

Below The gracious old house at Zwartkoppies is still perfectly preserved. *Centre* The bedroom at Zwartkoppies in which John Murray is said to have slept. *Bottom* The Zwartkoppies billiard room remains true to the interiors of its heyday.

Poltergeists and doppelgängers

Poltergeists are troublesome spirits that, out of maliciousness, spite or a cruel sense of humour, create a lot of noise, throw things around and generally cause a disturbance. Whereas most ghosts are place specific – they inhabit a certain location and can be seen by anyone who visits the place in question – poltergeists tend to persecute individuals and move around to do so. In the main, poltergeists are usually seen only by the individual plagued by their presence, though the physical manifestations of their acts can be observed by anyone in the vicinity. Although 'persecution' by a poltergeist can persist for years, in most cases it lasts only a few months at the most.

Scratches and scars

One of the most famous and well-documented cases of poltergeist activity in South Africa occurred at Rietfontein, a small town on the Namibian border, in 1992. Five teenage girls at the local secondary school began being 'attacked' by a spirit that lacerated their clothes and scratched their arms and legs, apparently with pins or similar. On more than one occasion, pins were actually driven into their legs.

Let there be light!

On Friday, 12 April 2002, this author, attended the opening night of the Johannesburg Mystery Ghost Bus Tour, organised and led by Mark Rose-Christie, South Africa's leading paranormal investigator. During the course of the evening, the tour visited The View, an old Victorian home in Parktown, Johannesburg, where the tour party were told about the ghost of Lady Cullinan, who is said to inhabit the property. At the very moment when the tour guide – in this instance, ex-*Police File's*, David Hall-Green, was explaining that Lady Cullinan was sometimes in the habit of switching off the hall light near the main entrance to advertise her presence, the light in question went off for no apparent reason.

The light switch, which was in full view of the author at all times, had not been interfered with. So how would one then explain what happened? The short answer is that one can't. The View is a relatively old house, so one could argue that the wiring may be suspect and that this could explain this rather strange occurrence. On the other hand, it could indeed have been Lady Cullinan who had made an appearance…

Right Contrary to popular thinking, ghosts do not traditionally haunt cemeteries, preferring places that tend to show more signs of life.

Did you know?

The word *poltergeist* is a German word that means 'noisy ghost', while the German word *doppelgänger* means 'double-goer'.

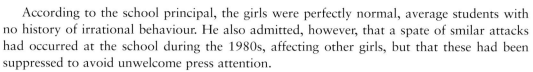

According to the school principal, the girls were perfectly normal, average students with no history of irrational behaviour. He also admitted, however, that a spate of smilar attacks had occurred at the school during the 1980s, affecting other girls, but that these had been suppressed to avoid unwelcome press attention.

The week the Rietfontein events hit the headlines, one girl's hair was mysteriously hacked off. She had also suffered a fit two weeks previously. Another girl had had her hair burst spontaneously into flame. A local priest who visited the school ruled out mass hysteria, however, and allegedly attributed the attacks to 'satan'. And after a few weeks, the 'attacks' ceased without explanation and have not been repeated since.

Doubles and doppelgängers

In general, most people assume ghosts to be spirits of the dead or dying, but there is evidence to suggest that they may also be manifestations of living people. A 'double', for example, is an individual who is seen by different people at different locations, but at the same time. A 'doppelgänger', on the other hand, is a special form of double where a double or copy appears near to the 'true' person and is seen doing exactly the same thing the 'true' person did a short time earlier. In other words, doppelgängers are rather like action replays that repeat a series or actions or an incident at a later time. Both doubles and doppelgängers are thought to be either death omens or out-of-body experiences that have been manifested either consciously or unconsciously.

Left Doppelgängers are, in fact, manifestations or 'ghosts' of living individuals.

The problem with poltergeists

In the 1970s, two English researchers, Alan Gauld and A D Cornell, carried out a computer analysis of 500 poltergeist cases that had occurred around the world since 1800. Their research showed that:

- 24% of poltergeist activity persisted for just over a year
- 58% were most active at night
- 48% included rapping sounds
- 64% involved the moving of small objects
- 36% involved the moving of large pieces of furniture
- 12% involved the opening and shutting of doors and windows
- 16% of the cases involved direct communication between the poltergeist and the subject.

They also established that where a specific person was being targeted by the poltergeist, it was most often a female under the age of 20. The Gauld/Cornell study also showed that, of the 500 cases under investigation, only 7 per cent were blamed on witchcraft and only 2 per cent on demons.[14]

The man who foretold the future

Nicolaas Pieter Johannes van Rensburg (1862–1926) had visions, extraordinary visions, and during his lifetime was accepted within the Boer community as a man possessed of the God-given ability to foretell the future. In fact, General JBM Hertzog allegedly stated that Van Rensburg 'lived in a constant maze of visions and symbols. Like somebody eternally twisting the tuning-knob of a wireless, hearing senseless noise and discord most of the time. Suddenly, the right wavelength is there and harmony comes over the ether.'[15]

For folk and fatherland

Van Rensburg was born on 30 August 1864, and grew up on his parents' farm, Rietkuil, near Ottosdal. When he was a boy, his mother would read him stories from the Bible and later on, when he worked as a shepherd on the farm, he would always take the Book with him when he went out into the veld. Allegedly, he read nothing else and, at the comparatively young age of 21, he was appointed as an elder of the NG Congregation Wolmaranstad. A year later, he married Annie Coetzee and together they raised 10 children.

According to his mother, Van Rensburg began to demonstrate his power of prophecy while still very young, but it was during the South African (Anglo-Boer) War of 1899–1902 that his power of prediction became more widely known. At the outbreak of the war in 1899, Van Rensburg and his brothers joined General Du Toit's commando and, during the early days of the conflict, they were witness to the burning of Boer farms and the killing of Boer families.

Traumatised by these events, Van Rensburg returned to Rietkuil to recuperate and it was during this period that the frequency of his visions increased dramatically. He then began to move from commando to commando, in an attempt to help the war effort in the only way he knew how: by foretelling the future.

Although Van Rensburg was not always able to decipher the precise meaning of the images that flashed into his mind, his predictions were often so accurate that his fellow burghers credited him with special powers and started to refer to him as 'Siener Van Rensburg', 'Die Siener' (the seer) and 'Die Profeet' (the prophet). In fact, it was a generally held belief among the Boers that God had sent Van Rensburg to assist them in their struggle against the British.

The red bull with the crippled leg

Van Rensburg made one of his most remarkable predictions to General De la Rey on the night of 6 March 1902. Six days earlier, Lieutenant-General Paul Methuen had led a British column out of Vryburg. He was moving against De la Rey's Boers and, with the help of a second British force led by Colonel Grenfell out of Klerksdorp, was hoping to trap his enemy in a pincer movement. On the eve of battle, however, Grenfell was still more than 30 miles away, his column having been harassed and delayed by a second Boer force led by General Van Zyl.

The night before the battle, De la Rey asked 'Siener' van Rensburg what the outcome of the fight would be. Historian Julian Orford[16] takes up the story…

Did you know?

South Africa had its own Nostradamus. His name was Nicolaas Pieter Johannes van Rensburg, and he is widely acclaimed as one of the most accurate soothsayers this country has ever seen.

Van Rensburg's visions

Siener van Rensburg's uncanny abilities earned him enormous respect among not only his own community, but also from some of the most highly regarded Boer commanders during the South African (Anglo-Boer) War, most notably Christiaan de Wet and Koos de la Rey, when his predictions pinpointed a number of enemy tactics before they had been excuted by the British military.

After the war, Van Rensburg returned to Rietkuil where he continued to receive visions. He predicted with amazing accuracy the death of General Koos de la Rey, the Boer Rebellion of 1914, the great influenza epidemic of 1918, the Great Depression, the victory of the National Party in 1924 and a number of other events.

His daughter, Mrs Anna Badenhorst, wrote down many of his later prophecies in two exercise books. Siener van Rensburg died on 11 March 1926 at the age of 62.

'The Prophet, who made a great name for himself during and after the war, had made several remarkably accurate forecasts of events to come, and De la Rey believed him to some extent, but never based his plans on what Van Rensburg said. De la Rey was strictly a tactician to whom the principles of war, of which he had never heard, came naturally. The "Siener" spoke of his latest vision in which he saw a red bull approaching from the direction of the town of Vryburg. He was eager and strong, his head and horns stood erect, and he was spoiling for a fight. However, near Barberspan the bull became weary, his head hung, and De la Rey should seize the opportunity and dehorn him. General Jan Kemp also asked the "Siener" what would happen. Van Rensburg said he had seen a red bull, which was running down a slope, suddenly turn about and stumble up again, with one crippled front leg – "*Een kreupel voorbeen*".

'The [British] column moved off in two divisions from Tweebosch on 7 March 1902, the ox-convoy starting at 3 am, escorted by Cape Police, the Yeomanry, all the Infantry and Lieutenant Venning's guns. The main column moved out at 4 am, escorted by the Cape Special Police, Ashburner's Light Horse, with one pom-pom forming the advance guard, and Dennison's Scouts and the Diamond Fields Horse the rear guard. Lieutenant Nesham's guns were with this column.

'By about 5 am, the head of the column had reached De Klipdrift on the Great Harts River, when the Boer attack opened on the rear-guard. The fire put down by Nesham's guns and the second pom-pom were effective for a while, but not for long. At 5.30 the ox-column was ordered to halt, and at 6 am the attack assumed serious proportions when, in addition to attacking the rear of the column, a movement was made against the column's right flank. Methuen, in accordance with previous arrangements, took post with the infantry. Major Paris, commanding the mounted troops, reinforced the rear while Methuen extended the infantry and brought Venning's guns into action. Lines of charging Boers, firing from the saddle, in extended order, disregarding the heavy fire directed at them, pushed forward. After a small measure of resistance, nearly all the colonial troops broke and fled...

'At about 9.30, Methuen was hit in the thigh. He dismounted and lay down next to his horse. It was hit, wounded a second time, and fell on him, breaking his leg. Colonel Townsend, the column's Principal Medical Officer, splinted Methuen's leg with two rifles, and was hit three times in rapid succession. The fight was over and surrender was inevitable...

The return of the red bull

'Methuen was sent to No. 13 General Hospital at Nourse Deep Mines on 23 March, and landed in England on 9 July. He was operated on later and parts of a bullet and bone splinters were removed. A second operation followed in 1903, after which his health improved. He returned to South Africa on 22 April 1908, as Commander-in-Chief Imperial Forces in South Africa; but this time he walked with a stick, to overcome a limp caused by the shortening of his right leg, a legacy from Tweebosch. He referred to it in his diary as 'a gait of my own' but nevertheless played golf into advanced old age.

"Siener" van Rensburg's strange prophecy concerning the red bull with a crippled front leg could hardly have been more accurate.'

Below Also known as the 'Boer Prophet' and Siener (seer) van Rensburg, Nicolaas Pieter Johannes van Rensburg's accurate predictions meant that many Boers believed he was a messenger sent by God.

When witchcraft fails

In 1918, Louis Tumpowski, a Jewish immigrant from the United States, was murdered by his common-law wife, Dorothea van der Merwe (or Kraft, as she was known at the time of her crime) and, as the tale unravelled, it became one of South Africa's most notorious crime stories, filled with mystery, intrigue – and witchcraft...

Kraft and Tumpowski – an itinerant general dealer whom Kraft had met when he visited her farm with supplies – had lived together for a time, but had separated, and relations between them were strained. To complicate matters, during their time together, Tumpowski, had obtained a legal claim to buy Kraft's property at a price that was well below the current market value. When Kraft realised that her ex-lover was intending to take advantage of this situation, she resorted to witchcraft to protect her interests.

She approached a local witch doctor named Jim Bird and asked him to provide her with a love potion, which she could use to snare Tumpowski, and later bend him to her will. She realised that this plan had failed, however, when Tumpowski reiterated his intention of

Wondering about witches?

Witchcraft has been a part of traditional African life for many centuries and the term 'witch' is generally meant to refer to individuals who are able to harm others through psychic means. These individuals, who are called *umthakathi* among the Zulu and *moloi* by the Sotho, are born with these powers; they are not abilities, it is believed, that can be learnt. Witch doctors, on the other hand, are specialists who attempt to counteract the powers of these witches.

In 1995, the Northern Province established a Commission of Enquiry into Witchcraft, Violence and Ritual Killings. In the commission's report, tabled in May 1996, it was stated that thousands of people in the province had been accused of witchcraft and had been driven out of their homes or had lost their property. It was also revealed that over 300 people accused of practising witchcraft had been killed by vigilante mobs over the previous 10 years. Those killed had been accused of 'shape shifting' themselves from human form into bats and birds, converting people into zombies and causing death and destruction by calling down lightning or using poisons.

In September 1998, the Commission for Gender Equality (CGE) convened a conference in Thohoyandou to address the issue of witchcraft-related deaths. In a subsequent report on the Conference entitled 'Witchcraft Violence Conference Report', which was published in March 1999, it was revealed that between April 1994 and February 1997, 97 men and 46 women in South Africa had been accused of being witches or wizards and that, in the first six months of 1998, 386 crimes had been perpetrated against suspected witches in the Northern Province alone. The crimes in question included murder, damage to property and assault, and were mostly committed against women between the ages of 55 and 72 years.

In July 2000, the CGE initiated a 'Witchcraft Roadshow' in the Northern Province, the aim of which was '...to raise awareness of the gendered and criminal nature of witchcraft violence and killings.' In the opening address at the launch of the Roadshow, the chairperson made the point that '...the majority of those fingered and accused of witchcraft were women... [and that the Ministry of] Safety and Security was, in general, concerned with the criminal conduct and lawlessness associated with witchcraft killings.'

Significantly, the South African Police Services is the only police force in the world to have a specialised unit dedicated to the investigation of Occult Crimes. This unit is based in the Limpopo Province.

taking ownership of the property. It was then that Kraft approached Bird a second time, this time demanding that he cast a spell, which would kill 'the old Jew'.

For magic of this strength, Bird explained, small personal effects (including a lock of hair) belonging to Tumpowski were required. Kraft obliged and Bird placed the items in a matchbox. After incanting a spell, Bird instructed Kraft to bury the matchbox beneath the threshold of Tumpowski's room. When he crossed the threshold, the spell would take effect and Tumpowski would weaken and die, Bird promised.

On to plan B

When it became clear that this attempt had also failed, Kraft decided upon a different course of action: she employed the services of Bird (for £100 this time), a certain Hermanus Swartz, and three local labourers to bludgeon Tumpowski to death with a knobkerrie. And so it was that Tumpowski was attacked and murdered in Kraft's farmhouse and his body buried outside.

Eventually, however, folk became suspicious about Tumpowski's continued absence and an investigation was eventually initiated by local police. But the going was slow, with very little evidence and every supposed 'lead' ending in failure, and it was only some two and a half years later that the body was discovered.

It was then that Jim Bird struck a deal with the police and was offered immunity from prosecution in exchange for turning King's Evidence. Dorothea Kraft and Hermanus Swartz were found guilty of the murder of Louis Tumpowski and later hanged at Pretoria Central Prison. The three labourers involved in the murder were acquitted for lack of evidence.

Dorothea Kraft thus became the first woman to be hanged in the Union of South Africa.

Above According to ancient custom and traditional beliefs, *sangomas* beat the drums to create the right environment for the ancestors.

Going… going… gone! One soul

On Tuesday, 28 May 2002, an article in *The Star* reported that Nathan Wright (24), an enterprising advertising web designer from Des Moines, Iowa, had put his soul up for sale on the Internet.

'It all started when I was selling normal stuff like a computer monitor and mouse,' Wright explained. 'You look around your house and say, "Well, what else could I sell?".' Somewhat more philosophically, he added: 'Hopefully, the buyer won't be someone who uses it maliciously. I'm really not worried about selling it, unless the devil has an account on eBay. I don't know, maybe that's something he's resorted to.'

Apparently, however, eBay were less confident because it subsequently withdrew the advert before the auction could go ahead. But, undeterred by his setback on eBay, Wright then moved across to Yahoo. In the end, the highest bid he received for his soul was a rather paltry $31 (R310).

Wright later said that selling his soul was also a way to get publicity for his online magazine, *Monkeycube.com*. The successful bidder, he said, will receive his soul in a tiny jar that 'may or may not have contained fudge'.

Did you know?

In 1997, the South African government passed the Suppression of Witchcraft Act, which banned both the practice of evil sorcery and most forms of traditional African healing.

The terror of the tokoloshe

According to South African sage, Credo Mutwa, the tokoloshe (or *hili*, as he is known in Xhosa) '...looks like a very nasty-looking teddy bear in appearance, in that it's head is like that of a fierce bear, but it has got a thick, sharp, bony ridge on the top of its head. The ridge goes from about the forehead to the back of its head, and with this ridge it can knock down an ox butting it with its head.'[17]

It is to avoid the wrath of this unpleasant creature, Mutwa explains, that Polynesians build their huts on stilts about one metre above the ground, the same height many black South Africans raise their beds on bricks above the floor.

Right A tokoloshe-type creature is found in the myths and legends of people around the world, and is often blamed for accidents, social disruption, lewd attacks and general mischief.

Did you know?

Although widely referred to in South Africa's oral tradition, the tokoloshe is not particular to local cultures of southern Africa. Known by other names in other traditional cultures, the tokoloshe appears to be just as common further north on the continent.

In a *Weekly Mail & Guardian* interview with Lazarus Sentsho in 1995, tokoloshes were described as creatures that '...look like a baboon or a short, hairy man with a long penis. It is also reputed to have an insatiable sexual appetite and in order to satisfy this lust, prowls around at night to rape unsuspecting women'.[18]

This unpleasant creature, says Sentsho, '...do(es) the work of witches... It is widely believed that anyone who owns one of these creatures has the ability to acquire great wealth, at the expense of others.'[19]

Tokoloshes, which are able to enter any residence through a crack in the door, are also believed to have an uncanny power called *mashoshapansi*, which means 'to make it go under'. *Mashoshapansi* gives them the ability to extend their penises to any length and send it underground into the genitals of a sleeping or unsuspecting woman.

For this reason, the tokoloshe is frequently associated with illicit and hedonistic sex and is often blamed for the socially disruptive consequences of these activities. When a woman loses interest in her husband, for example, it is often interpreted as being the result of rape by the tokoloshe.

Many people are extremely afraid of tokoloshes, which they believe are sent by witches to bring death, while others merely consider them troublesome. Some believe that one should not bring water into the house at night as the tokoloshe will enter at the same time. Similarly, the tokoloshe loves to steal food, but only if it is unsalted because these little creatures are thought to hate salt. Generally speaking, children are thought to be safe from them. In fact, tokoloshes reputedly like to play with children.

Tokoloshes are also reputed to have the ability to make themselves invisible, which they achieve through the use of a small charm – sometimes allegedly in the form of a pebble, which they carry with them.

Despite differing perceptions regarding the appearance and habits of these small creatures, there does appear to be consensus about one thing: they are the cause of much distress for all those whose paths they cross.

Tokoloshes make the news

One of a number of incidents involving a tokoloshe was reported in the *Sunday Times* on 27 January 1987. The article described the experiences of the Ramlall family, who lived in Northdale, Durban. The Ramlalls claimed they were being persecuted by a paraffin-spitting tokoloshe that created havoc in their home by starting fires. In the end, the Ramlalls were forced to employ the services of a *sangoma* to rid their house of its presence. This the witch doctor allegedly did by trapping the small creature in a bottle, sealing the top and throwing him in a nearby river.[20]

Tokoloshe meets its match

In another *Sunday Times* story – 'Muti didn't work for these suspects'[21] – it seems that a tokoloshe, which was assisting a gang of car thieves carry out their nefarious activities, was forced to flee the scene of a crime when confronted by the police. According to the article, the drama began when the police stopped a suspected stolen car in Groutville near Stanger. When they searched the vehicle, the officers found a skull on an enamel plate in the boot. Inside the skull was a piece of meat, which the men said was an offering to satisfy the hunger of a tokoloshe. Apparently, the three shocked occupants of the car had shaken their heads in disbelief when they realised that their *muti* had let them down. (They later admitted that the skull and meat had been blessed by a *sangoma* and had been given to them specifically in order to elude the authorities.)

Above 'Muti' is a broad term used to refer to indigenous medicinal plants and to preparations made by sangomas. Indigenous plant medicines are critical to the wellbeing of the vast majority of South Africans.

'This time our *muti* was stronger,' said Stanger police sergeant Esau Smith. 'It seems that the tokoloshe had fled the scene in fear, leaving the three to face the music. I am not mocking the power of the tokoloshe, but this is definitely one time that the power of the law was much stronger,' he said.

Sergeant Nicholas Xulu, another police officer involved in the incident, remarked that the tokoloshe had no power over him because he was religious: 'I am God-fearing and no *muti* or tokoloshe is able to take control over me.'

Stanger police spokesman Michael Harris said that the arrested men's *muti* had evidently 'crossed the floor to the opposition'. 'It could have been the *muti* talking,' he added, 'because the suspects immediately fingered nine other people who were part of a car-theft syndicate operating in the Stanger area. Thanks to the three alleged thieves – and their *muti* – we have been able to bust one of the biggest car-theft rackets in the area.'

Tokoloshes, it seems, may have remarkable powers, but this doesn't necessarily enable them to avoid the long arm of the law. The three alleged car thieves appeared in the Stanger magistrate's court on eight counts of car theft and were remanded in custody, and the skull – suspected to have been dug up from a grave – was handed to Stanger mortuary.

Tokoloshes work on white people too!

An article published in the *ZimbabweBiz* magazine in June 2000 suggests that white people should also beware the dreaded tokoloshe.[22] In this article – 'Tokoloshe attack – curses work on white Africans too!' – it was said that a woman of 'Portuguese descent' had accused her neighbours' domestic workers of causing both the run of bad luck she had recently suffered, and the loss of some personal items.

Despite the fact that the woman's accusations were met with derision, she had insisted on calling in a *sangoma*, who had agreed that there was something 'not quite right' about the house and had promptly conducted a cleansing ceremony intended to send the tokoloshe back to whoever had called it up.

Shortly afterwards, so the story went, a domestic worker in the employ of the woman's next-door neighbours, unexpectedly fell ill and asked to return to her rural home, while the domestic worker at the house on the other side of the woman's property had also suddenly left the area without warning. Both these events, it was suggested, were tokoloshe related.

Another story in the same article, described the case of an office manager who was convinced that her black bookkeeper was trying to destroy her with *muti*. The 'proof' was that the office manager had suffered a 'near-fatal, freak car accident, her husband had lost his job, and the business she had built up from nothing... [had] suffered unreasonable reverses'.

The article further suggested that it was 'fairly common practice' among some white Zimbabweans, 'who are generally thought by blacks to have no knowledge of such things', to summon *sangomas* to reverse or remove curses.

Endnotes

1. John and Anne Spencer, *The Encyclopedia of Ghosts and Spirits* (1992), BCA, p. 22.
2. Ibid., p. 22.
3. Margaret Williamson, *Haunted Corners – South Africa's Own Ghost Stories* (1993), Cape Town: Ad Donker, p. 20.
4. John and Anne Spencer, op cit, p. 216.
5. Eric Bolsmann, *Ghosts of Pretoria* (1997), Pretoria: Be My Guest Publishers, p. 8.
6. Ibid., p. 8.
7. Ibid., p. 11.
8. Margaret Williamson, op. cit., p. 106.
9. Ibid., p. 106.
10. Andrew MacKenzie, *Hauntings and Apparitions* (1982), Heinemann, p. 8.
11. Eric Bolsmann, op. cit., p. 40.
12. Ibid., p. 43.
13. Interview with the author.
14. Rosemary Ellen Guiley, *The Guinness Encyclopedia of Ghosts and Spirits* (1995), Guinness Publishing, p. 262.
15. Siener van Rensburg, www.geocities.com/Athens/Rhodes1266/historical-Prophet.htm
16. Julian Orford, 'The Dust of Conflict' in *Military History Journal,* Volume 5, Number 4, The South African Military History Society.
17. Interview with Credo Mutwa, reported in *MetaTech* (16/5/2002), http://metatech.org/credo
18. 'The little creature with a big appetite', *The Weekly Mail & Guardian* (27/12/1995).
19. Ibid.
20. Rob Marsh, *Unsolved Mysteries of southern Africa* (1994), Cape Town: Struik Publishers, p. 72.
21. 'Muti didn't work for these suspects', *Sunday Times* (4/4/1999).
22. 'Tokoloshe attack', *ZimbabweBiz* Magazine (3/6/2000).
23. Jan Knappert, *African Mythology* (1995), London: Diamond Books, p. 8.

The spirit of Africa

Although Western culture often tends to dismiss Africa's religious heritage and belief systems as 'primitive' or 'primal', spiritual practices on the continent are remarkably sophisticated, very often echoing similar concepts that had, in fact, developed separately in the northern hemisphere.

'African religions,' as Jan Knappert states in the introduction to his book *African Mythology*[22], 'are intricately complex systems of thinking, in which the beliefs, myths and cosmology of an ethnic group are interwoven with their moral code and rules of behaviour, into an infinitely variable organism of living religious ideas and actions.'

Indeed, similar concepts of good and evil, angels and demons exist in both Western and African belief systems. In southern Africa, the tokoloshe is a devil in male form who, among other things, has sexual intercourse with women in their sleep. In the West, the tokoloshe goes by another name – an incubus...

Scams and the Underworld

Sir Walter Scott's words, 'O, what a tangled web we weave, when first we practise to deceive', are a chilling reminder of the an underworld most of us would prefer to ignore. But criminals and confidence tricksters come in all shapes and sizes and colours and they live among us. Often as not, the crimes they commit are quickly forgotten – except, of course, by the hapless victims. There are, however, exceptions to the rule. These are the crimes that stand out from the crowd. The ones that we remember because they are unusual or uncanny...

A public spectacle

In the early hours of the morning of 4 January 1842, a shot and a scream rang out from the house of Jan and Anna Rabie in Cradock Street, Graaff-Reinet. The commotion awakened the Rabies' two maids, who rushed into the house to find a hysterical Anna Rabie cradling in her arms the dead body of her husband. A gun lay across his chest.

'He is dead,' Anna wailed. 'He has killed himself.'

Anna Rabie, neé Buitengracht, was born on 13 November 1810. Although she came from a humble family, she was well known throughout the district for her great beauty and, at a young age, she married Jan Rabie, a wealthy local farmer who owned a number of properties in the area.

Rabie, however, was often away from home in order to tend to his varied business interests elsewhere and it was during these frequent absences, at least according to the gossips in the town, that Anna first earned a reputation for having a number of 'men friends'. And one name in particular came up again and again when the goings-on in the Rabie household came up for discussion: Johannes Barend Liebenberg, a hunch-backed widower with three children.

Evidence suggests, however, Jan Rabie knew of his wife's infidelity. According to Jan's brother, Jan had, on one occasion, come home to find Anna and Liebenberg in the bedroom together and had subsequently moved out of the marital home for a few days. He had only returned after Anna had begged him to. Whether this apparent remorse on Anna's part was genuine or not is open to question, but return he did, and life in the Rabie household seemed to go back to normal. With hindsight, however, it now appears that this period was merely the lull before the storm, that Anna was playing the dutiful wife because she and her lover were planning a murder. The scheme they had hatched was simplicity itself: Anna would drug her husband with a sleeping draught and Johannes would shoot him. Together, they would make the killing appear as a suicide.

Did you know?

The only public hanging of a woman in South Africa occurred at Graaff-Reinet on 8 July 1842.

Following the clues

Johannes Liebenberg was first questioned by the police the day following the death of Jan Rabie. At first, he denied any knowledge of the crime or even of being in possession of a firearm, but he was soon proved to be lying.

Firstly, he had left a clear trail of footprints from the crime scene to his own front door and it was these 'crooked footsteps' – a reference to his disability – that had led the police to him. And a shop owner, Mr C G Osche, remembered supplying Liebenberg with a firearm and bullets a few days previously.

'It was last Friday, New Year's Eve, when I had shown him guns,' Osche told the police. 'He bought lead and lent my bullet mould.' Osche also recalled that Liebenberg had wanted a gun, 'that could shoot someone dead.'

Below Convicted of the murder of Jan Rabie, Anna Rabie and Johannes Liebenberg were hanged outside the Graaff-Reinet prison on 8 July 1842.

The police were able to match the bullet taken from the victim to three more bullets found inside Liebenberg's house. All four of the bullets had minute scratches etched into the cases and these marks, it was later established, had been made when Liebenberg had asked one of his employees to 'smooth down' the bullets on a stone because they were 'too rough for his liking'.

Police investigators were also able to establish that Liebenberg had sent one of his servants to deliver a sleeping draught, which he had obtained from a local doctor, to Anna. (After the murder, Anna buried this sleeping draught under a tree but was spotted by a neighbour, who subsequently informed the police. When this evidence was revealed at the trial, it proved especially damaging to both accused.) And if that wasn't enough, the police also discovered some of Anna Rabie's love letters in Liebenberg's pocket.

With little or no difficulty, the authorities had thus established the three critical factors that link the criminal to the crime: motive, method and opportunity.

Confronted by all the evidence against him, Liebenberg eventually confessed.

'It is true – I committed the murder,' he said, 'but only after she had talked me into doing so.' On three consecutive nights, Liebenberg explained, he had hidden outside the Rabies' bedroom window. Inside the house, Anna had drugged her husband and had then held a candle near his head in the bedroom so that Liebenberg could see the target more clearly. On the fourth night, Anna had called him to the window and shown him her husband sound asleep in bed.

'There's the dog,' she said, 'shoot him now.'

When he hesitated, she became angry: 'Johannes, if you don't shoot him now, I'll take the gun and shoot you!' – at which point Liebenberg had pulled the trigger. After that he had run back to his house.

When told of Liebenberg's confession, Anna also admitted to her part in the murder, though apparently with a tinge of disappointment.

'I did not know he was such a coward,' she said.

During the trial that followed, there would be suggestions that Anna Rabie acted only out of calculated self-interest and that she held no real affection for her husband. All she really wanted was to do, the prosecution would argue, was to lay her hands on her husband's fortune.

Hanged by the neck until dead

The trial of Anna Rabie and Johannes Liebenberg began on 10 May 1842 and lasted three days, after which the 27-man jury retired for a mere 20 minutes before delivering a guilty verdict for both accused. The judge then pronounced sentence: both would hang by the neck until dead, and the hanging was scheduled for 8 July 1842 – in full public view.

According to contemporary accounts, on the morning of the execution a large crowd gathered outside the prison where the two condemned prisoners were being held. The atmosphere was somewhat festive and many of the onlookers had brought picnic baskets to watch the spectacle.

Just before 8 am, the two condemned prisoners were fetched and transported to the gallows sitting atop their own coffins. It was a crisp morning and Anna was wrapped up against the chill.

She was the first to hang, but only after Jan Rabie's brother had first tied a length of string around her ankles and over the hem of her dress to prevent it billowing up when the trapdoor opened, thus protecting the convicted widow's modesty. Liebenberg was hanged immediately afterwards.

Did you know?

In the Cape during the 18th century, it was a point of law that a prisoner could not be hanged until he or she had confessed to the crime with which he or she had been charged.

After the verdict of guilty had been been passed down by the judge, Anna had asked the judge if she and her hapless lover could be buried side by side, but this wish was denied. Anna Rabie and Johannes Liebenberg were finally buried on opposite sides of the Graaff-Reinet graveyard.

Justice for all

In the centuries before Anna Rabie and her lover were hanged for the cold-blooded murder of Jan Rabie, it was as much a part of the judicial procedure to torture the accused as it is today to cross-examine a witness. In many instances, putting the accused to 'the question' usually occurred in the presence of the judge and the Court.

A favourite method was to tie 50-pound weights to the big toes of the accused and then, after fastening his wrists together with a rope, pass the rope over a beam above his head and haul him up off the ground.

Judges were also not averse to imposing the harshest of sentences when they felt the need to do so. In the Cape Court of Justice in 1732, for example, a European sailor who had been found guilty of murdering a free black woman and wounding a slave, was informed: 'The prisoner shall be hanged with the knife with which he has committed the crime above his head, his dead body to be taken from the place of execution to the outside and rehanged there and left exposed until destroyed by the air and the birds of heaven.'[2]

There was also the unusual case, in 1672, involving four mutinous sailors who had rebelled while employed to build the Castle of Good Hope. Unable to establish whom the ringleaders were, the Court decided to make use of a lottery. Sentence was thus passed that the four prisoners be '...condemned to draw lots for life or death'[3], and the two who drew the lots of life were to be scourged and sentenced to many years of hard labour, while those who drew the lots of death were 'to be punished with the halter' (hanging).'

Inevitably, men were treated more harshly than women and, in turn, black prisoners more harshly than white prisoners. A white man found guilty of theft, for example, was likely to be flogged and imprisoned, or at worst transported to New South Wales in Australia, whereas a black man who committed a similar crime, was usually hanged.

In the early 18th century, a white woman had apparently conspired with her black lover to murder the woman's husband. Both were sentenced to death. The woman, however, was sentenced to be half choked, allowed to recover, then 'scorched' and finally strangled to death. Her accomplice was impaled on a stake, where he was left to die slowly.

According to contemporary reports, he was given a bottle of arrack – an alcoholic drink – at which point the onlookers called out that he would get drunk. The doomed man, however, said that it did not matter since he now sat so firmly that he could not fall over.[4]

It allegedly took the unfortunate prisoner more than two days to die.

Men who murder

The vast majority of murders – some 85 per cent – are committed by men and, if one takes into account the number of murders committed by men in times of war or civil unrest, then the percentage of killings committed by women is negligible. What is more, of those killings that are carried out by women, almost two thirds are arguably acts of self-defence, committed out of desperation in order to escape a long and abusive relationship. This is not to suggest that women don't commit murders that are motivated by greed or jealousy, but rather that these types of crimes are exceptions to the rule.

Why men are generally more aggressive and violent than women is uncertain and research in this regard remains sketchy. The evidence does indicate, however, that male aggression is not due to genes, hormones or chromosomes, but rather as a result of a complex combination of a number of factors, including the socialisation process.

Although reliable statistics are extremely difficult to obtain, the best estimates suggest that in South Africa – like the rest of the world – between one-in-four and one-in-six women who are married or in a long-term relationship are being physically abused by their male partners. This pattern of male-to-female abuse has led American criminologist Enid Bagnold to conclude that 'a murderess is merely a woman with a temper'.

Phillipus Swarts and the Kruger Millions

The name of Phillipus Swarts, who fought against the British in the South African (Anglo-Boer) War as a member of Ben Viljoen's Johannesburg commando and was eventually hanged for murder, has often been linked with the so-called Kruger Millions. Swarts' treasure and the Kruger Millions, are not, however, one and the same – although they do have a common denominator: both 'treasure troves' were allegedly buried at more or less the same time, and in more or less the same place.

The legend of the Kruger Millions originated in the spring of 1900 when, at best estimate, about £500,000 worth of mainly 'raw', unminted gold was transported from Pretoria to Machadadorp and later Lourenço Marques (now Maputo) in order to prevent it falling into the hands of the advancing British army. What happened to this gold is fairly well documented: it was shipped to Europe, with the money raised from its sale being used to continue the struggle against the British.

Nevertheless, even as Kruger's Millions were leaving the country, several stories began to do the rounds. One such story was that not only was a great deal more than £500,000 worth of gold removed from Pretoria, but also that a large quantity of this gold had been hidden somewhere on the Highveld.

In fact, so many people were convinced of the existence of the Kruger Millions that, following the cessation of hostilities, the authorities began issuing permits to anyone wishing to search for buried treasure. Indeed, so great was public interest in the matter that official forms were printed to expedite the application process. Aspirant treasure hunters were expected to declare their intention in writing and, in the event that any treasure was found, agree to give two thirds of the find to the government. The man given the task of issuing these permits was Colonel H W Trew of the South African Police.

To discover the origin of Phillipus Swarts' treasure trove, however, we need to go back a few years before the South African (Anglo-Boer) War began...

Opposite En route to join the Boer forces, Phillipus Swarts and a companion known only as 'Jones' stumbled across what is popularly thought to be the long-lost Kruger Millions. In fact, the treasures were that of a local chieftain known as Qugunyan.

A fortune in gold and diamonds

According to an account published in the January 1941 edition of South African Police magazine, *The Nongquai*, a 19th-century tribal chieftain named Qugunyan, who lived to the east of the Lebombo Mountains, was in the habit of demanding tribute from those members of his tribe who crossed into what was then known as the Transvaal to find work. This tribute often took the form of a gold nugget or a quantity of gold dust from those who worked in the goldfields, or a diamond from those who worked in Kimberley.

Qugunyan acquired a considerable fortune in this way, but around the turn of the century, his situation changed rather dramatically when he fell out of favour with his Portuguese overlords and they sent an army against him. On the eve of battle, Qugunyan hurriedly sent his wives and his fortune to safety in the care of his most trusted *indunas*. Their destination was the Pilgrim's Rest area, where Qugunyan's relatives lived. The following day – or so the story goes – Qugunyan was killed in battle and his kraal torched.

The real Qugunyan?

In all likelihood, the story of Qugunyan is based on the exploits of Gungunhana, a warrior chieftain who resisted Portuguese imperialism in the region during the last decade of the 19th century. In July 1897, Gungunhana was captured by the Portuguese and although he was not killed during this action, his power base was destroyed, effectively ending his rule. Also perhaps significant is the fact that Gungunhana was then head of the Gaza state, which had been established in the 1830s by Soshangane and held hegemony over the Tsongas, from whom Gungunhana demanded tribute.

Unfortunately, Qugunyan's wives and the *indunas* he had sent along with them to protect them, seemed to fare little better. Whether because of hunger or thirst (a devastating drought gripped the entire region that year) or because of they were ravaged by wild animals is unclear, but the small band of refugees died – or were killed – in the bush and Qugunyan's fortune was lost.

Enter Phillipus Swarts...

In about November 1900, Swarts – described as a 'large man with a black beard' – and a companion named Jones were riding through the bush near the Olifants River en route to rejoin their commando, when they came upon human remains. Dismounting to investigate, they also found among the bones raw skin bags containing diamonds, gold and coins. These they took with them and later buried them alongside what Swarts called a 'cream of tartar tree' near the junction of the Blyde and Olifants rivers. After Swarts had made a rough map of the site in his pocket book, the two men continued on their journey and finally rejoined their commando.

Shortly afterwards, both Swarts and Jones fought in the Battle of Renosterkop against a brigade of British troops led by Major-General Arthur Paget. Jones was killed during the skirmish – from a bullet in the back, it was alleged – but Swarts survived, only to be captured shortly afterwards. He was sent to St Helena, where he remained a prisoner of war until the war ended in 1902. He then returned to Johannesburg.

Tracking the treasure

While he was living in Johannesburg, Swarts formed a friendship with a man named Van Niekerk, to whom he eventually confided the story of the buried treasure. And, in the winter of 1903, the two men decided to seek out the treasure together. They travelled north to Pietersburg – where they employed two black servants – and then set out for Leydsdorp and, later still, the small mining settlement of Phalaborwa, near the Selati River.

When Colonel Trew heard that Swarts and Van Niekerk were looking for treasure without a permit, he promptly dispatched two of his soldiers, Corporal Bonsfield and Trooper Ferguson, to find them.

It is around this time that accounts begin to differ. According to Laurence Green's *A Last Glance at the Kruger Millions*, Swarts was tracked through the bush, eventually apprehended and taken back to Pietersburg, where he was imprisoned. It was during this pursuit, Trew maintains, that Bonsfield and Ferguson found a human skull, with a bullet hole through it, and some other remains, including a ring bearing the initials 'C. v. N'.

In *The Nongquai* account, a slightly different version is told.[5] According to 'Justice', the author of the article, the last time Van Niekerk was seen alive was one afternoon when he and Swarts walked off into the bush together. This was after the small band of treasure hunters had set up camp at a location Swarts had indicated was near to where the treasure was supposedly hidden. At dusk, just as darkness was about to settle, the two men in camp heard a rifle shot. Not long afterwards, Swarts returned, saying that he had wounded a buck, which had run off, and that he and Van Niekerk had been separated while trying to track the animal to ground.

When Van Niekerk failed to return by the following morning, the three men set out to find him. Eventually, they discovered a note pinned to a tree, allegedly from Van Niekerk. The note said that he (Van Niekerk) had become disillusioned with the expedition and was returning home.

Did you know?

A king's ransom in gold coins and uncut diamonds is said to be hidden somewhere near the junction of the Olifants and Blyde rivers in Mpumalanga.

Once they had discovered that Van Niekerk had 'deserted' them, Swarts apparently made a half-hearted attempt to find the treasure himself. Finally, maintaining that the task was indeed impossible because the landscape had changed too much over the years, the treasure hunter abandoned the search and the three men returned to Pietersburg, where they disbanded and went their separate ways.

In *The Nongquai* version of the story, Mrs Van Niekerk, who was living in Johannesburg, later saw a woman friend of Swarts wearing a ring she recognised as one belonging to her husband. When confronted about the ring, the woman said that she had been given it by Swarts, at which point Mrs Van Niekerk took her to see the Chief of the Criminal Investigation Division (CID) at Marshall Square.

As part of their investigation into the matter, the police subsequently sent a search party into the bush near the Olifants River and eventually found the skeleton of a European with a bullet hole in the skull. On the basis of this evidence, Swarts was arrested and charged with murder, and a trial date was set.

The pieces of the puzzle

Despite the differing accounts, both stories nevertheless have an unusual number of elements in common. What is, in fact, not in dispute is that Van Niekerk and Phillipus Swarts set off together to search for the hidden treasure of the Kruger Millions. Both of the accounts also agree that Van Niekerk's remains were found in the bush with a bullet wound in the skull, and that a ring belonging to Van Niekerk proved incriminating evidence against Swarts.

It was, however, while Swarts was waiting for his trial date to come around that the story takes yet another strange twist. Just before the case came to court, Colonel H Mentz, Swarts' lawyer, began asking for money towards the defence costs. After some delay (during which time, it is said, Swarts arranged for someone he knew to return to the Olifants River area), a strange meeting took place.

According to Colonel Trew, Mentz was asked to go to a particular place in Pretoria at night, where – or so the story goes – he would be given enough money to cover Swarts' defence. At the meeting, a 'dark stranger' handed Mentz a black bag containing a large amount of cash, including a number of the coins that appeared to have been buried in the ground for some time.

Swarts was subsequently found guilty of murder and sentenced to death by hanging by the judge, Sir James Rose-Innes, who would later describe the trial as 'the most remarkable murder trial in my experience'. While on death row, Swarts allegedly summoned one of the CID officers with whom he had become acquainted and told him the story of the treasure, which, he insisted, he was determined to keep out of the hands of the 'damned British'. He also apparently handed over the map he had drawn, saying that the vast majority of the treasure still lay buried.

Later that year, so legend has it, the same officer went on a 'hunting trip' in the Lowveld, but apparently without any success. Trooper Ferguson, who had first arrested Swarts, was of the opinion that Swarts had split the treasure into small amounts, which he had distributed at various points near the Mozambique border. (It was presumably one of these caches that had been used to pay for Swarts' defence.)

The interesting fact is, if either account is accurate, then Swarts' treasure is still lying hidden in a hole in the ground, probably somewhere in what is today the Kruger National Park, just waiting to be unearthed…

A shot in the dark

At about 10 minutes to seven on the night of Tuesday, 18 April 1989, Johan du Plessis was sitting in the stand at Ellis Park Stadium watching a rugby game, when he felt a tremendous blow to his chest. When he looked down, blood was pouring from a wound in his sternum: he had been struck by a stray bullet that had been fired into the air by a man standing on the balcony of an apartment building well over a kilometre away.

Du Plessis was immediately rushed to hospital, where a surgeon removed a bullet from his chest. The police then opened an attempted murder docket. It was at this point that ballistics experts from the South African Police Service's ballistics unit, based at the L P Neethling Building in Pretoria, were called in.

At the beginning of the investigation, all the police had to go on was the number of the seat in which Du Plessis had been sitting and the bullet that had struck him, but in less than three days, detectives from Jeppe police station had arrested the person responsible and had confiscated the weapon he had used.

The investigation begins

In theory, the science of ballistics involves examining tool marks, calculating angles and forces and applying basic laws of physics. In practice, things are rarely quite as simple as this would suggest.

In the case of Du Plessis, after examining both his chest X-rays and the bullet itself, forensic experts were able to determine that the bullet that had struck him had been fired from either .38 special or a .357 magnum. Also significant was the fact that the bullet was largely undamaged. This suggested that when it had struck Du Plessis, it had been more or less at its maximum range, with less energy left to penetrate and deform.

Microscopic examination of the bullet by forensic experts revealed that it had a groove system described as 'six grooves to a right-hand twist' – in other words, the gun that had fired the bullet had six rifling grooves in the barrel, causing the bullet to spin clockwise as it travelled through the air.

Although it is not always possible to identify the make of gun involved from this kind of evidence, the police believed that the weapon in question was probably an Astra revolver.

A matter of maths

According to ballistics expert Superintendent Jan de Waal, in order to calculate both distance and direction it is necessary to work backwards from the point of impact. 'To calculate distance, it is necessary to know the probable range of the firearm in question. Both a .38 special and a .357 magnum have a maximum range of about 1500 metres when discharged at an angle of about 29 degrees above the horizontal. This means that that if you fire one of these guns into the air, the bullet is likely to travel about a kilometre and a half before it falls to earth.

'Of course, most people fail to understand the damage that can be caused by a stray bullet over large distances. A .22 rifle, for example, is dangerous for about 1500 metres, but something like an R1 rifle can kill from up to four kilometres away.

'The preliminary evidence indicated that whoever had fired the shot that had struck Mr Du Plessis, had been standing well over a kilometre from the stadium. Even so, the terminal velocity of the bullet in question was about 79 metres per second on impact, which is still sufficient to kill a person. Mr Du Plessis is very lucky to be alive because the speed at

Did you know?

Ballistics is an extremely precise science involving the study of projectiles, the characteristics of flight dynamics and firearms.

which a projectile must travel to penetrate skin is about 50 metres per second and to break bone is around 65 metres per second.'

Having established the calibre, probable type and range of the firearm in question, the next task was to determine the direction from which the bullet had been fired.

Du Plessis had been seated in seat number 244 in row A on the lower level of the eastern side of the stadium and he was able to indicate to the police the way in which he had been sitting when he had been struck by the bullet. Using this information, forensic experts were able to determine probable angles of incidence, indicating the likely direction from which the bullet had been fired. It was eventually calculated that he had been shot from a vertical angle of between 60 and 80 degrees, with a horizontal offset of 20 degrees to the right, with a possible 10 per cent degree of error to left and right of the line thus created.

This data was then fed into a computer and, using a ballistics programme, detectives were able to pinpoint more accurately the area from which the shot had been fired. The probable areas identified for each of the respective calibres – a .38 and .357 – included Hillbrow, Berea and Yeoville.

In this way, the total area from within which weapons of the two calibres in question could have been fired was reduced to less than half a square kilometre. (The actual area calculated was 0,42 square kilometres.) The most probable area for a .357 magnum was limited to 0,098 square kilometres.

Making an arrest

With the probable area from which the shot was fired now reduced to a few city blocks, police officers from Jeppe police station then began the arduous task of conducting door-to-door enquiries.

Below By studying the trajectory of the bullet that hit a spectator watching a rugby match at the Ellis Park Stadium, police were able to pinpoint the Madison Square apartment from which it was originally shot.

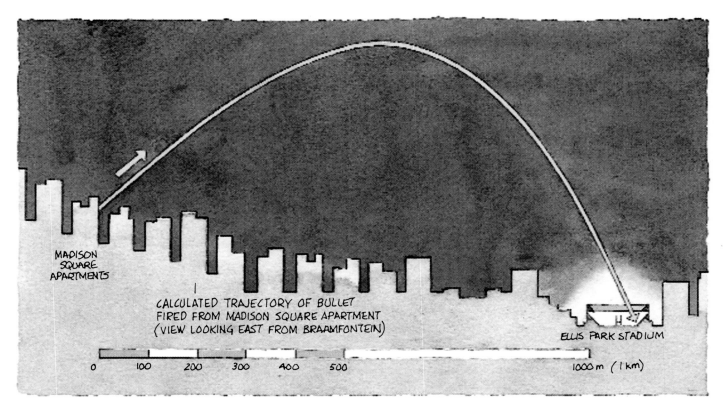

MADISON SQUARE APARTMENTS

CALCULATED TRAJECTORY OF BULLET FIRED FROM MADISON SQUARE APARTMENT (VIEW LOOKING EAST FROM BRAAMFONTEIN)

ELLIS PARK STADIUM

0   100   200   300   400   500   1000 m (1 km)

Bullets and ballistics

The word 'ballistics' is derived from the Latin *ballista*, meaning 'to throw'. Modern ballistics, however, is divided into three separate disciplines: internal ballistics, external ballistics and terminal (or wound) ballistics.

Internal ballistics is concerned with the interaction between the barrel of the gun or firing mechanism and the projectile, and is a study of the marks that are transferred from one to the other during the shooting process. These marks include rifling grooves in the gun barrel, which are transferred to the bullet or shell, and the marks left by other machined parts such as the firing pin, extractor or breechblocks, which also carry individual characteristics that are, in turn, transferred to the cartridge case. Microscopic examination of these marks allows an expert to connect a bullet or cartridge to a specific weapon.

In order to link a specific bullet to a specific firearm, it is necessary to obtain a 'test' bullet. This is done by firing the suspect gun in question – usually into a water-filled 'shooting' tank, which is used to 'catch' the bullet. The marks – called striations – on the 'test' bullet are then compared to those on the bullet under examination.

Most modern gun barrels are rifled, meaning that a spiralling groove is cut into the gun barrel. The ridges between the spirals are called 'lands', and it is the lands that cause the bullet to spin and that cut into the bullet as it travels down the barrel. The only firearms that do not leave striations are smooth-bore guns like shotguns and antique weapons of the flintlock type.

Internal ballistics is essentially the study of tool marks, which explains why ballistics experts are sometimes called upon to examine pliers, bolt cutters, cut wire and even teeth marks.

External ballistics is the study of projectiles in flight and, in this regard, it is important to remember that bullets do not fly in a straight line, but follow a parabolic trajectory that becomes more and more curved as range increases and velocity decreases.

Sophisticated equipment is used to determine both the muzzle velocity of a firearm – either of a particular manufacturer's weapon type, or of a specific bullet from a specific weapon – and the velocity and performance of a bullet after it has left the barrel. With this information, it then becomes possible to calculate how far a bullet would go, the energy it generates and at what speed it would be travelling at any point in its trajectory. This information can be of vital importance when an expert is called upon to give evidence in a court of law.

The ballistics unit of the South African Police Service also makes use of a Hadland camera, which is a state-of-the-art photographic system capable of capturing a bullet in flight. The equipment is able to take five photographs in five-millionths of a second. Using the Hadland camera, it is also possible to see what a bullet does as it strikes a target or after it has struck a target. In this way, the effect of the bullet on the target and the target on the bullet can be determined.

The Hadland camera used by the SAPS is one of only two used by forensic units worldwide. All other cameras of this type are housed in artillery units belonging to the military.

Terminal ballistics is the study of the effects of a bullet or projectile on its target. When the target is human, this is often referred to as wound ballistics. Contrary to popular belief, it is not always easy for an inexperienced examiner to determine that a wound has been caused by a gunshot and an experienced examiner will always be on the lookout for misleading signs. When a bullet strikes a body, it often makes both an entry and an exit wound. The entry wound is usually a neat, round hole that is smaller than the bullet and there is often relatively little blood loss. More obvious damage occurs around the exit wound. However, where a weapon has been fired close to or against the skin, a star-shaped or cruciate wound results. Once again, to the inexperienced eye, this can look more like an exit than an entry wound.

Below The underground firing range at the LP Neethling Building in Pretoria is a showcase for the SAPS ballistic unit, which has a worldwide reputation for excellence.

They were looking for someone who had heard gunshots being fired in the area on the night in question, and within 48 hours they interviewed a resident in the Madison Square apartment building who claimed to have heard shots being fired from one of the flats higher up in the building at the time the rugby match was being played. Further inquiries led the police officers to apartment number 1101, where two men were arrested, one of whom confessed to the crime.

That same day, Friday, 21 April 1989, microscopic examination proved that the test bullet and the bullet that had been retrieved from Du Plessis' chest had both been fired from the confiscated weapon.

The two men concerned were both found guilty of attempted murder and each fined R500, while the owner of the weapon was declared unfit to possess a firearm.

Broadsheet ballads and bullets

In 1794, Edward Culshaw was found murdered with a bullet in his head at Prescott, in Lancashire, England. The surgeon who examined the body discovered a wad of paper in the wound. The writing on the paper was still legible: it was part of a broadsheet – an early newspaper – containing an extract from a popular street ballad of the time.

(The muzzle-loading flintlock pistol used in the murder was loaded by pouring gunpowder down the barrel, and tamping it down with a wad of paper or cloth to prevent it spilling out. Then the musket ball would be pushed into the barrel and held in place by a second piece of paper, rammed on top of it. It was one of these pieces of paper that was carried into the wound inflicted on the victim.)

Suspicion subsequently fell on an 18-year-old youth named John Toms, who was known to own a firearm similar to the type used in the murder. When Toms was arrested and searched, an edition of the same broadsheet – but with a small section torn out – was found in one of his pockets. When the frayed edges of the scrap of paper that was removed from the wound was fitted to the broadsheet found on Toms, they matched exactly.

On the basis of this evidence, Toms was found guilty of murder and hanged.

The first time scientific evidence linked a specific bullet to a specific weapon was in 1889 when the French forensic scientist, Alexandre Lacassagne, gave evidence in what was called the Eschallier Affair. Lacassagne showed the court that the bullet removed from the victim and the gun barrel belonging to the suspect both had seven grooves. This evidence helped the police obtain a conviction.

Dr Paul Jeserich, a Berlin-based forensic scientist, was allegedly the first person to use actual striation comparison, using a test-fired bullet, while giving evidence in a murder case in 1898.

The first bureau of forensic ballistics was set up in New York in 1923, and the British police first established a forensic laboratory at Scotland Yard in 1934, while the South African Police first set up a forensic laboratory in 1971.

Below Usually a loud and lively venue for enthusiastic rugby supporters, Ellis Park Stadium in Johannesburg was the setting of one of the most baffling 'crimes' investigated by local police in recent years.

Free money!

October 2001

Dear Sir

I am the widow of the late General Sani Abacha who died about two years ago in Nigeria... I and the entire family wish to let you know that we inherited our father's wealth among others is cash sum of US$136,000,000 from bogus and inflated contracts. His intention was to open a bank account in Switzerland... Now my problem is to negotiate with a foreign partner who is reliable and honest... as I do not want this money here and I do not want to lay hands on this money until I have concluded all arrangement [sic] to move this money to a safe over-seas bank... We have decided to give US$36,560,000 to anyone who wish to help my family finalise this project... We plan to transfer the money by awarding a non-exis-tent contract from the Nigerian Petroleum corporation to you. You provide a very vital account into which the fund will be transferred... In 1995, Paolo Luigi, a director of an Italian firm, made away with our funds. We need a more reliable person to deal with this time around.

The follow-up letter

I should like to re-assure you that this transaction is 100% risk free and legal. Modalities have been put in place to ensure the safe, fast and immediate release of US$36,560,000. I have been given permission to allow you to carry out the release procedures ... We promise to give you 20% of the total contract sum for your cooperation, confidentiality, trust and honesty... Please find below an official release letter from the Office of Debt Reconciliation Committee, Federal Ministry of Finance, Nigeria.

(Letters sent to a *Mail & Guardian* reader. Reported in the *Mail & Guardian*, Saturday, 27 October 2001.)

What is the 419 Scam?

The 419 Scam is a so-called advance-fee fraud. An advance fee fraud occurs when a victim is coerced or induced into paying out money in the expectation that he or she will receive a much larger payback shortly thereafter. The common term – 419 scams – takes its name from Section 419 (Chapter 42) of the Criminal Code of the Federation of Nigeria and Lagos, which states that 'any person who by any false pretence and with intent to defraud obtains from any other person anything capable of being stolen, or induces any other person to deliver to any other person anything capable of being stolen is guilty of a felony and is liable to imprisonment...'.

In simple terms, the object of the exercise for the tricksters is to use greed and the lure of easy money to persuade unsuspecting victims to hand over large amounts of cash in the belief that, in return for facilitating a money-laundering deal, they – the victims – will receive a commission amounting to millions of dollars. The reality is that people who are taken in by this worldwide, multibillion-dollar scam end up losing their money. They also risk being kidnapped and tortured, and possibly even murdered.

South Africa's growing importance

There is evidence to suggest that South Africa is rapidly becoming a favoured location for international crime syndicates operating this scam. This is partly due to the country's modern and effective communication and banking systems infrastructure, and partly because it is strategically situated on the major drug-trafficking routes between the Far East, the Middle East, America and Europe. Also, South Africa's somewhat chequered history as a pariah state is often used as an excuse for the secrecy and subterfuge that is an integral part of this kind of advance-fee fraud. And finally, of course, the perpetrators of these 'deals' are, for the most part, themselves African, and are thus more able to blend in with the general population.

Nigerian fraud syndicates in South Africa operate in small cells usually consisting of five or six individuals. Each member of the cell has certain unique skills and each cell, which usually operates in a given geographical area, forms part of a loose association that has both national and international links. In the main, the cells operate independently and can change their complexion and character from day to day. In other words, they are not part of a strictly controlled and structured organisation such as the Mafia or the Chinese Triads, although they can work together when necessary. Sometimes, for example, a number of cells combine resources and money in order to bring a shipment of drugs into the country, which they later divide up and distribute among themselves.

In fact, it is this fluidity that makes catching the fraudsters so difficult. The situation is further complicated by the fact that the crime usually occurs in a country other than that in which the victim lives. This means that when a case comes to court the victim has to be brought into the country to testify. This can be costly and the outcome uncertain and for this reason both law enforcement agencies and the victims themselves have proved reluctant to take this step.

Current estimates suggest that at around four or five people are enticed to South Africa every week in the hope of making easy money in this way – one of the downsides of South Africa becoming part of the global community.

The modus operandi

The 419 Scam involves bringing victims to South Africa or, less commonly, sending South Africans overseas. This is how the system works:

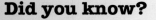

Did you know?

Almost every week, countless victims – both from South Africa and abroad – are being conned out of millions of dollars by a Nigerian-based confidence trick called the 419 Scam.

Step 1

The fraudsters contact a potential victim, usually by mail, fax or e-mail. Choosing whom to send a letter to can be as arbitrary as going through names in a telephone book or scouring the Internet for likely choices, but the letters are distributed in a variety of ways to millions of potential victims. Sometimes, hundreds of letters are sent out simply to get one 'bite'.

In one way or another, the letters all say the same thing: the writer is an asylum seeker, a prominent government figure or official, and he or she is in possession of a vast amount of money that needs to be transferred to a save haven, but lacks the facility to do so. In return for assistance, the person involved will receive a commission amounting to millions of dollars, pounds or Euros. No mention is made of the advance fee payments that will be required to facilitate the deal.

Step 2

When a potential victim replies, the criminal will immediately make contact, either by fax, or e-mail, and ask the victim for particulars such as his or her telephone numbers, bank account details and so on. After this, the victim is likely to receive a telephone call. The caller will explain the process of the 'deal' and stress the need for both urgency and secrecy. The criminal will also raise the issue of an advance payment to facilitate the deal. This money, it will be explained, is required to pay lawyers' fees, to bribe corrupt officials, to obtain the necessary documents or for a variety of other reasons.

Step 3

Letters, faxes and official-looking documents are sent to the victim to support the criminal's story and request for payment. These documents, which can include letters from law-enforcement agencies, the South African Reserve Bank, lawyers, the police, top government officials and so on, appear authentic and are highly convincing.

Step 4

By this stage the victim has bought into the 'deal' hook, line and sinker. The urgency of the matter rapidly increases: suddenly, there is a chance that the deal will fall through or be cancelled if the victim does not come up with an 'advance' immediately. One way or another, he or she hands over the money, usually between $5000 and $100,000.

Step 5

The victim will be invited to travel to South Africa, if a foreign national, or out of South Africa, if a South African national. This journey is necessary, it is explained, either to open a non-resident bank account overseas, or to conclude the deal by signing all the relevant documents. The criminals will also go so far as to arrange visas – sometimes fraudulent, sometimes genuine – where necessary. All expenses are paid by the victim with the promise that he or she will be refunded once the 'deal' has been concluded.

Step 6

On arrival in the foreign country, the victim will be met at the airport and taken (at his or her own expense) to a hotel, where they will stay until the 'deal' is concluded – or they run out of money.

During this time, the victim will usually meet the person who initiated the 'deal' or a 'delegate' sent in his place. They will discuss details of the transaction, the programme for his or her stay, any 'fees' still outstanding, how the victim's money will be transferred out of

Mustapha Sule
Lagos-Nigeria

STRICTLY CONFIDENTIAL & URGENT

D Jacobs

I got your contact from the British Chamber of Commerce, and they recommended you as an honest and trustworthy person. Based on this recommendation, I decide to contact you on behalf of Mrs Mariam Abacha, wife of Nigerian late Head of State. When her husband was alive, the head of state, I was made personal assistance [sic], charged with the responsibilities of handling her personal business and finances. Before the death of her husband, she strictly moved the sum of US$15.5m (Fifteen Million Five Hundred Thousand Unites States Dollars) in the custody of a reputable security company in Amsterdam, Holland.

Now her husband is dead and she can not travel out of Nigeria yet, to avoid the present democratic government from raising eye brow [sic] on her. She has instructed me to contact a reliable person abroad to go to Amsterdam, Holland, and secure the sum of US$15.5m, which she personally deposited at the security company in Holland.

Mrs Mariam Abacha want you to secure the funds in Amsterdam, and subsequently invest it on her behalf in your country with the trust that you will not dissappoint or let her down.

For your assistance in this project you will be entitled to 20% of the total sum involved. Note that this cash transaction is only between Mrs Mariam Abacha and I, therefore it is a risk-free business.

There is nothing to bother about in this transaction.

The fund are [sic] already in a vault waiting for your arrival.

If you are interested in this project, kindly contact me immediately through the above e-mail address for further details before your departure to Holland.

Note also, that this project requires a lot of secrecy and confidentiality. Therefore you must keep this project secret all times.

Looking forward to hearing from you to begin a good business relationship.

Sincerely yours

Mustapha Sule

Personal Assistant to Mrs Mariam Abacha

the country, travel arrangements, and a host of other matters that seem relevant. The victim is also likely to meet with a series of 'lawyers', 'bank managers', and possibly even a 'Governor of the Reserve Bank', all of whom will be at pains to convince him or her that the deal is indeed genuine.

Step 7

Using a variety of excuses – bribing corrupt officials, paying holding fees, etc. – the victim will be milked of any remaining money in their possession. An official-looking receipt of some kind will be given for each 'payment' to 'prove' the legitimacy of the transaction.

Step 8

The criminals will provide 'reasons' why the victim needs to transfer more money into the country. This might be for chemicals, in the case of a Black Dollar Scam or demurrage fees, for the release of a fictitious vehicle that has been 'delayed' by the authorities.

Step 9

To further convince the hapless victim of the authenticity of the proposed deal, he or she will be taken to a bank to open a non-resident account. The criminals may even forge a transfer-confirmation slip to prove that the money in question is being transferred to the victim's new bank account.

The criminals only disappear once they are absolutely convinced that the victim has no more money to hand over.

Mr Jacobs' story

Mr Jacobs (not his real name) is a businessman living in Johannesburg. This is his story...

'In 1999 I received an e-mail out of the blue from someone calling himself Mustapha Sule. At the time, I owned my own small engineering company. Business was quite good, though I wasn't making a fortune, so when I got a letter inviting me to make $4 million I was naturally interested. Sceptical, but interested.

'More out of curiosity than anything else, I replied to the e-mail, expressing some interest in the matter, and asking for more information. A few hours later, I got another e-mail, also from "Mr Sule". This second e-mail explained in more detail about how Mrs Abacha had managed to spirit millions of dollars out of Nigeria following the death of her husband, but that she couldn't access the money herself because she was being watched by the Nigerian secret service. That was why she needed an "unknown" to act as an intermediary on her behalf. The problem was, the letter explained, that the authorities were getting close. If she couldn't get hold of a willing accomplice soon, the entire fortune was likely to be confiscated. If I was willing to help, the letter continued, I'd get 20 per cent commission, nearly $4 million, of the money that was being "rescued"!

'I still wasn't convinced, but after thinking about it for a couple of hours, I sent off my contact details. After all, what did I have to lose?

'Two hours later, I received a phone call from Mr Sule himself and it was probably that phone call, more than anything else, that won me over. The person I spoke to was obviously well educated and sounded completely genuine, and I have to admit I was impressed by his straightforward, businesslike manner.

'During the course of the conversation, he explained that a "problem" had arisen. That morning, he said, he'd received notification that one of Mrs Abacha's personal assistants had gone missing in South Africa and it was thought he had been kidnapped by the Nigerian secret police. It was only a matter of time, he reckoned, before the authorities found out about the money. In order to prevent this happening, some money was needed to pay off a corrupt South African official.

'I still had doubts, so Mr Sule faxed me a copy of a letter from the Nigerian Reserve Bank, confirming the transfer of US$15.5 million to a bank based in Holland and a letter from the bank in Holland acknowledging receipt of the funds in question.

'These convinced me that the deal was genuine and I offered to pay. I suddenly thought I'd stumbled onto a virtual gold mine. An hour later, I went to an office of the Western Union and transferred R10,000 to an address in Cape Town.

'Two hours later, Mr Sule phoned me again. "Can you fly to Amsterdam tonight?" he asked. I couldn't believe what I was hearing. "You can't be serious," I remember saying, but he was serious. And he was very agitated this time because he had just found out that the whole "deal" was in jeopardy because of a greedy bank official who wanted paying off. If we didn't get some cash to the official concerned, he said, then all of Mrs Abacha's money would be sent back to Nigeria.

'I could tell from his voice that there was a crisis. Suddenly I realised that If I didn't act fast, my $4 million would be lost for ever.

'"How much is needed for the bribe?" I asked.

'"$10,000. Can you get that much?"

'"Yes," I said. That was when I agreed to fly to Holland.

'I flew to Amsterdam the following night, taking with me $10,000 in traveller's cheques I had raised by taking a loan against my business. But, then, what was $10,000 when I was going to earn almost $4 million?

'True to form, two of Mr Sule's colleagues – Mr Harrison and Mr Mtibi – met me at the airport and whisked me off to a hotel they had booked. Both men were extremely well spoken and, from the way they talked, I could tell that they were high-ranking ex-government officials from Nigeria.

'Unfortunately, of course, there had been yet another slight problem, Mr Harrison explained as we were driving through the city: the corrupt official I had come to pay off had decided to up his price.

'Naturally, I was eager to get the whole thing over with quickly, but they both reassured me that everything was going to be alright and that all I had to do was stay at the hotel and do exactly as they told me. If I did that, they said, within three days I'd be back home in South Africa – $4 million richer.

'The next day, I had a meeting with a man calling himself Mr Tembo, who said he was Mrs Abacha's lawyer. He explained to me exactly how the "deal" was going to work, but the first thing I had to do was give him $5000 to bribe a custom's officer who had "got in the way".

'Twenty-four hours later, Mr Harrison and Mr Tembo took me to a bank to cash my remaining traveller's cheques and to open a non-resident account. Two days later, the two men came to the hotel again. This time they were very excited.

'According to Mr Tembo, the "deal" was going to happen that afternoon. Then he explained that the reason for the delay had been that the government official who was bringing the bank clearance certificate from Nigeria had been delayed in Lagos. He was arriving that afternoon and all we had to do was pay him off, then transfer the money into my account. Then it was simply a case of transferring the money – minus my 20 per cent commission, of course – to Mrs Abacha's account in Switzerland.

'That was when I handed over the $5000 and the two men left for the airport, or at least that's what they told me. They phoned me an hour later to say that everything had gone off smoothly and that they were on their way back to my hotel to take me to the bank to do the transfer – and that's the last I heard of them.

'The next morning, I telephoned the South African Embassy because I needed money to pay my hotel bill and get back to South Africa. I know I was stupid, but I don't consider myself a gullible person. It just all seemed so genuine, all the documents I was shown seemed authentic, and I was blinded by the thought of all the money I was going to make. What more can I say?'

Cellular science

Every individual is made up of about 100 billion cells and, in the 1940s, it was discovered that every cell contains a protein surrounded by a nucleus made up of a substance called nucleic acid. There are two types of nucleic acid – RNA (ribonucleic acid) and DNA (deoxyribonucleic acid).

In 1953, James Watson and Francis Crick, 'solved' the DNA code and showed that the DNA molecule has a thread-like structure consisting of a double helix of interlocking spirals that contain the 'building blocks of life'.

It was not until the 1980s, however, that Dr Alec Jeffreys, working at the University of Leicester in England, developed a method of accurately comparing DNA from different individuals. This process came to be popularly known as DNA fingerprinting.

DNA analysis is a complex, labour-intensive process and, under normal circumstances, it takes a laboratory about 12 weeks to determine a 'finding' that can be presented in a court of law. The cost of this process is also substantial. In 2001, for example, the South African Police Service spent over R27 million in order to conduct about 12 000 DNA analyses, at an estimated cost per analysis of about R1300.

The automated DNA analysis system, called the DNA Criminal Intelligence Database (DCID), will change all that. Not only will the new system reduce costs by about 25 per cent, it will also be much quicker. Once the system is fully streamlined, for example, it will be possible to process about 120 000 DNA analyses a year, a tenfold increase on present capacity. (This figure can be doubled to 240 000 per year if a second DNA Sequencer is brought into the system.)

The DCID system will also be able to provide a preliminary 'finding' within two hours, although it is expected that the normal turnaround time per analysis will be in the region of one week.

The DCID system is built upon two main pillars. The first pillar is a crime index, which contains samples collected from crime scenes and victims, and the second pillar is a reference index that contains DNA samples from suspects and victims.

Below The DCID computer promises to revolutionise DNA analysis. The machine, a world first, was developed by South African scientists for the SAPS.

The reference index will contain an ever-growing database that contains DNA samples from convicted felons, against which it is possible to compare new samples taken from crimes under investigation. This information can be used to confirm that a suspect was present at the scene of the crime, or, where there is no suspect, to identify an individual whose DNA is recorded in the reference index and whose DNA was found at a crime scene.

To facilitate the process, medical officers and district surgeons are already placing blood samples directly into a small 'container' called a Marshal cassette – yet another innovation by South African scientists – which has been designed to fit directly into the DCID machine.

Only a small 'target area' of the DNA taken from an individual is used for analysis, and for this reason scientists are not able to declare in a court of law that a specific sample came from specific individual with absolute certainty. However, the chances of any individual – with the possible exception of identical twins – sharing the same DNA profile is infinitesimal, normally in the region of one in 10 billion. For this reason, DNA evidence is usually accepted by the courts as being both compelling and conclusive.

According to a police spokeman from the South African Police Service's Commercial Branch, Mr Jacobs was extremely lucky only to lose $10,000.

'One has to realise,' the police officer explained, 'that the criminals who commit these crimes are consummate actors, extremely professional and very, very convincing. Nothing is left to chance.

'Take the initial contact letter, for example, which is full of grammatical errors. Some victims take this as evidence that the sender is poorly educated or of low intelligence and they assume that, if the deal is genuine, that they are going to be able to easily outwit the writer! This is exactly what the fraudsters want you to think.'

'In the case of Mr Jacobs, there is no "Mr Sule". He is just one of the many names the particular fraud cell that contacted Mr Jacobs uses. Also, there is every likelihood that if the police were able to track down the premises from where the e-mail was sent, all they would find was an empty room containing a chair, a table, a fax machine, a computer and literally nothing else.

'What most victims also fail to realise is that the people who carry out these scams can be extremely dangerous. If they have the victim in their clutches and they feel that he or she is getting cold feet and is about to pull out of the deal, some groups are quite prepared to resort to kidnapping, torture, extortion and even murder to get what they want. The fact that Mr Jacobs only lost money suggests that he was duped by one of the "good" cells, meaning essentially a non-violent group.

'It's all about taking control and psychology, you see. That's why the fraudsters create a sense of urgency, causing the victim to go through a roller coaster of emotions so that they can get him or her to do what they want. That's probably why they kept Mr Jacobs waiting at the hotel for four days. Not only were they checking him out to make sure that he was a legitimate businessman and not a police plant, but by keeping him on the wrong foot all the time, they were virtually ensuring his compliance.

'The criminals dupe their victims into acting irrationally by dangling a million-dollar carrot under their noses. And, like Mr Jacobs, many victims only see the money they may make and forget everything else. It's like greed takes over and makes them suspend their natural caution. I have had cases where the victim has spoken to me during the course of the scam, but still goes ahead and gives away his money – even after I told him that he was being conned.

'In the normal course of events, it's almost impossible to explain how an intelligent, astute or cautious individual can act so irrationally, but one has to remember that the victims are dealing with professionals who play on one of our most powerful human frailties: greed.'

The Black Dollar Scam

The so-called Black Dollar Scam is often used in concert with the 419 Scam. In this case, however, victims are led to believe that a fortune in American dollars has been smuggled out of Nigeria, but have been stained with a black dye to mislead the authorities. All that is needed to return the money to pristine condition is to 'clean' the notes using a chemical solvent. To this end, victims are often taken to a 'security company', replete with 'guards' and 'offices' and so on, where the money is being stored. Here they are shown a trunk full of 'black dollars'. They also witness the cleaning by a 'chemist' of one of the stained notes. A genuine American dollar bill is thus revealed before their eyes.

The usual scam is for the victim to buy a quantity of the 'cleaning solvent' – which usually turns out to be nothing more than coloured water or something similar – and the 'bank notes' themselves are, of course, merely pieces of paper dyed black.

Stealing stones

It is not possible to determine the exact scale of diamond theft in southern Africa. This is simply because no one knows for certain how many diamonds are present at any given location, so no one can be sure how many diamonds may or may not have been stolen.

De Beers bases its estimates on the amount of stolen goods recovered both from their own mines and by the Diamond and Gold Branch of the South African Police Service and similar law enforcement agencies in Namibia and Botswana. Another indicator is the fact that each mining operation should produce a certain quantity of predetermined grades. If certain quantities of these grades are not met, then the diamonds have either been lost in the recovery process, or – more likely – stolen. A third indicator is what is presented to the buyers at diamond-buying centres around the world.

Although diamond theft at mines has always taken place, the extent of the theft is known to have increased dramatically in the mid-1980s, when a number of sophisticated syndicates

Right Just one of the inventive methods smugglers have developed for stealing diamonds from South African and Namibian mining areas.

Did you know?

South Africa is the top supplier of gem diamonds in the world, producing more than 10 million carats a year.

began operating and there is now considerable evidence to suggest that mine employees are being coerced into engaging in illegal activities – despite extensive security measures, including physical searches and low-dosage X-rays.

Out of sight, out of mine

There have, of course, been an inordinate number of highly creative methods for getting the stones out of the mines. One individual, for example, was in the habit of taking a taking a small lunch box to work with him every day, which, of course, was never searched since he was taking it into the mine. It was eventually discovered that the lunch box contained a homing pigeon! The bird had a small harness attached to its back, into which the thief placed a number of stones, and, when no one was looking, he released the bird. When he returned home, the bird would be waiting for him with the diamonds.

Another thief smuggled sections of a crossbow into the mine where he was working. After he had assembled the weapon, he would attach stones to the bolt and fire it out of the mine, where an accomplice would be waiting.

Pebbles in the pocket

Once the stones are out of the mine, they often have to be smuggled out of the country. Again, a number of sophisticated – and, indeed, not-so-sophisticated – methods have been used. In Ian Fleming's book, *Diamonds are Forever*, for example, James Bond conceals a small fortune in diamonds inside his Dunlop 65 golf balls. In the real world, smugglers can be equally creative.

Diamonds have been smuggled in tubes of toothpaste, aerosol cans, various cosmetic containers and a host of other receptacles. One German courier was picked up at Bombay customs when it was noticed that he appeared to be walking on tiptoe: this was because a parcel of diamonds had been hidden inside the hollowed-out soles of his shoes!

In Tanzania, a well-known bird exporter was convicted of smuggling diamonds from the Mwadui mine when it was discovered that he was feeding the diamonds to the birds he was exporting. And possibly the most bizarre method of all was in the cavity of a false eye, and involved a young woman who had lost an eye in a car accident.

Big business

Diamond theft and diamond smuggling is very big business and, in some countries, has the potential to seriously undermine the national economy. In South Africa, diamonds make a significant contribution to the economy, but in Botswana, they dominate the economy, bring in up to 88 per cent of foreign earnings and generate around 30 per cent of gross domestic product – double the next most important sector of the economy, agriculture. In Namibia, diamonds contribute around 10 per cent of gross domestic product.

Endnotes

1. The author gratefully acknowledges the kind assistance of the following individuals in the compilation of this chapter: Superintendent Jan De Waal; Inspector Francois Bakker; Superintendent Sicro Schambriel; Captain H Koekemoer of the South African Police Service Museum; Captain Tertius Stapelberg; Inspector Alwyn Olivier; Senior Superintendent Joe Smith of the South African Police Service's Forensic Laboratories.
2. Oliver Jenkins, 'Strange and terrible sentences', *The Nongqai*, October 1938, p. 1052.
3. Ibid.
4. Ibid.
5. *The Nongqai*, January 1941, pp. 25–27.

Proudly South African

Even in the most ancient of times, Africa was widely acknowledged as a remarkable place, one of extraordinary achievements and equally extraordinary people. As long ago as the first century AD, the renowned philosopher Pliny the Elder declared: '*Ex Africa semper aliquid novi* – There is always something new out of Africa.' Here, we look at some of South Africa's more celebrated sons and daughters.

Little Foot makes a big impression

In 1994, Dr Ronald Clarke discovered four articulating homonid foot bones while looking through a box of miscellaneous fossil animal bones that had been excavated from the Sterkfontein cave in the late 1970s. These bones had been overlooked, but Clarke believed that he had stumbled upon a new species of hominid that walked on two legs, but also spent a significant amount of time climbing trees.

Clarke's interpretation was initially rejected by a number of scientists, but in 1997 he found a further eight bones from the same individual while examining a box of fossil monkey bones from Sterkfontein. One of the bones – a shin bone – appeared to have been broken by blasting, and this suggested that the individual in question might still be found inside the cave. At this point, Clarke asked Stephen Motsumi and Nkwane Molefe, two preparators working at Sterkfontein, to search the cave for a matching piece of bone. Within two days, the two men found the contact with the rest of the bone in the ancient infill of the cave. Clarke and his team then began the task of excavation. The rest, as they say, is history…

Top right The study of Little Foot's skull has revealed much about the ancestors of humankind.
Below Little Foot's footbones had been stored for over 20 years before they were rediscovered by Dr Ronald Clarke in 1994.

Little Foot comes back to life

This find was merely the latest in a long line of world-famous discoveries associated with Sterkfontein, but Little Foot – as this creature was affectionately called – was different. He was, in fact, special because of the completeness of the specimen and because evidence coming from this individual indicated that there had been a tree-climbing lifestyle and one involving upright walking about 3,3 million years ago.

'What makes Little Foot unique,' says Clarke, 'is that this is the most complete *Australopithecus*, or ape man, ever found. We have the left arm and hand, the head and both lower legs from thigh to ankle. For the first time ever, we have a skeleton with full dentition, with the lower jaw still attached, and in anatomical position. This means we can see what kind of limb bones go with what kind of skull.

Left Little Foot's arm bones were found in breccia. The hand, with its long thumb and relatively shorter fingers, is more like that of a modern human than of an ape.

'All we have to find are the backbone, pelvis and right arm and we will have the whole thing. And we know the rest of the skeleton is there: the missing sections have just sunk down to a lower section of the infill.

'Little Foot is also able to tell us about the creature's behaviour and locomotion. The hand is like that of modern human with long thumb and relatively short fingers, unlike apes, which have long fingers and a short thumb.'[1]

Little Foot and the evolutionary record

Dr Clarke continues: 'It is important to keep in mind that in the far, distant past there were many more species of ape than there are today. This means that the kind of ape from which we evolved may not necessarily be similar to those we know today – chimpanzees, gorillas, orang-utans and gibbons.

'We know that homonids evolved from some kind of ape, but we're not sure which one. All we have are these intermediate creatures that we call ape men. We use this term because they have some ape-like features, such as a small brain and prominent jaws, but they also have human-like features, such as the cusp pattern of the teeth, smallish canines and an upright posture.'[2]

The story of evolution is complicated by the fact that there were so many species of hominid or ape men. These include *Paranthropus robustus*, which lived at the same time as

Did you know?

The discovery of Little Foot, mankind's ape-man ancestor discovered at Sterkfontein, near Johannesburg, is still regarded as one of the most important archaeological finds in the world.

Homo habilis, but was a more specialised, heavily built creature, and *Homo ergaster* ('man who works'), while both species are associated with the manufacture of Acheulean stone tools. *Paranthropus* is not, however, directly related to the human species but was rather a specialised side-branch.

As Dr Clarke points out, one of the problems is that we only have what we find, and we only find where the fossils have been exposed, usually by erosion or human development. All that can be said at present is that all these creatures have human-like qualities and that they are our extinct relatives and more closely related to us than we are to apes.

Below Although we may never know the precise appearance of *Paranthropus robustus*, modern scientific discovery leaves little doubt as to its features.

The stars of Sterkfontein

Sterkfontein valley, which includes Sterkfontein caves, Swartkrans, Kromdraai, Gladysvale, Driemolen and Coopers, is one of the most important sites in the world for the recovery of fossils and stone tools relating to our ancestry and, as such, was finally declared The Cradle of Humankind World Heritage Site on 2 December 2000. It was the first place where an adult ape man was discovered in 1936 by Dr Robert Broom, and it is also the place where the greatest number of *Australopithecus* remains have been unearthed since then, including the remains of *Homo ergaster*, who lived about 1,6 million years ago and is thought to be modern man's direct ancestor. It is said that *Homo ergaster* was responsible for making the first stone tools in the early Acheulean period.

Two million years ago, Sterkfontein was a subtropical environment that was an ideal habitat for early hominids: the area was dotted with caves, which provided shelter, there was an abundant supply of animals that could be hunted or scavenged, and water was plentiful. Evidence emerging from excavations in the area suggest that a new biological species may have evolved in the region between 2,6 and 2,8 million years ago. It was this 'new' species of *Australopithecus africanus* that began to display more human-like characteristics, but whether this creature eventually evolved into modern man remains contentious.

The skulls of Sterkfontein

The Sterkfontein site is the longest-running archaeological dig in the world and has been a site of continuous excavation since 1966. Over the years, thousands of fossils have been

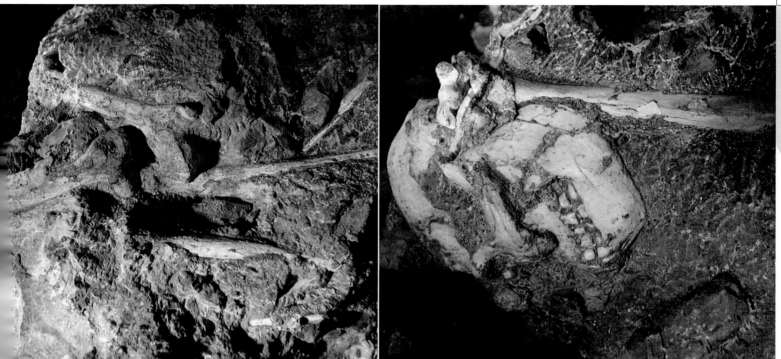

discovered there – including ancient plant remains, the remains of extinct mammals and at least four types of early hominid.

It was at Sterkfontein in 1936 that Dr Robert Broom made his first find when he unearthed parts of the face, upper jaw and cranium of a hominid that was similar to the infant ape-man skull found at Taung 12 years previously by Professor Raymond Dart.

At the turn of the 20th century, miners on the site used dynamite to blast out lime-rich deposits. After the lime had been removed, dumps of breccia – rock formed from broken fragments of other rocks, cemented firmly together – were left behind, which had no commercial value. It was in these dumps that the first fossils were found.

Broom named his find *Australopithecus transvaalensis*, putting it in the same genus as *Australopithecus africanus*, the name given by Dart to the so-called Taung Child.

But then, in 1937, Broom made a second significant find. This was a fragment of infant jawbone that he considered so different to the Taung Child that he changed the genus of this hominid, giving it the name *Plesianthropus*.

Ten years later, Broom uncovered a well-preserved skull of what he thought was a female *Plesianthropus*. 'Mrs Ples' – as the newspapers of the time referred to this find – remains the most complete skull of *Australopithecus* yet found.

The ape man *Paranthropus robustus*, discovered at Swartkrans in 1948 by Robert Broom and John Robinson, had a flat, sloping face, a low forehead and powerful jaws, which it used to crush and grind berries, fruits, roots and bulbs. It is not, however, an ancestor of *Homo sapiens*, although it did live at the same time and in the same areas as some of the early hominids from whom *Homo sapiens* evolved.

Paranthropus robustus probably became extinct about one million years ago, and fossils of this creature are very common in the Swartkrans area, where it appears the species was heavily preyed upon by big cats.

Top left The leg bones of Little Foot have revealed much about how it walked, leading to accurate comparisons with human abilities. *Above* The finding of Little Foot's skull has also allowed previously unexplored avenues of human anatomy to be explored with far greater accuracy.

Footprints in the sand...

Nahoon Beach in East London is where the world's oldest footprints of modern man are to be found. And unlike the footprints found at Laetoli in Tanzania in 1978 by Dr Mary Leakey, these footprints were made by modern humans, who were our direct ancestors.

The East London footprints – suspected to have been made made by a young person, possibly an adolescent – are thought to be about 200 000 years old and were first discovered in 1964, but it was not until 34 years later that their true age was established by Dr David Roberts of the Council of Geoscience in Cape Town, using a dating technique called Optically Stimulated Luminescence testing, which is thought to be accurate to about 10 per cent within a range of 100–200 000 years. (Radiocarbon dating had previously suggested the age of the footprints at about 29 000 years.)

In an interview with the *Sunday Times* on 8 November 1998, Dr Roberts is quoted as saying: 'These footprints are extremely important scientifically as they form part of a sequence of prints elsewhere in Africa showing human evolution. Unlike fossilised bones, the footprints give clues as to early man's activities along the coastline, which must have been an attractive source of food.

'People 200 000 years ago were more robust and stronger because they lived in a hostile environment. Let's just say that if this person sat next to you on the bus, you'd get quite a fright at their appearance.'

In fact, the East London find followed hard on the heels of another discovery of fossilised human footprints made by Dr Roberts at Langebaan lagoon a year earlier. These, also made by an anatomically modern human, were found in a sand-dune-turned-rock and were thought to be about 117 000 years old, the oldest human footprints on record at the time.

According to Dr Lee Berger, a paleoanthropologist at the University of the Witwaterand, who announced the find, the footprints have other implications: 'Whoever left these footprints has the potential of being the ancestor of all modern humans... If it was a woman, she could conceivably be "Eve".'[3]

To paleoanthroplogists, 'Eve' lived somewhere in Africa between 100 000 and 300 000 years ago, and carried a particular type of mitochondrial-DNA genetic material that is passed on only through females. Scientists measuring the range of variation in mitochondrial-DNA in different populations today have concluded that we all descend from one common female ancestor, whom scientists have christened 'Eve'.

'It is highly unlikely, of course, that the actual "Eve" made these prints,' Berger went on to say, 'but they were made at the right time on the right continent to be hers.'

Roberts also discovered some Stone Age tools in underlying rock in the vicinity of the footprints. These are thought to have been crafted by the people who left the footprints and constitute evidence of modern human activity during the period 100 000 to 300 000 years ago, which otherwise has a very limited fossil record.

By contrast, the oldest human footprints ever found in Europe are thought to be only between 25 000 to 27 000 years old. These footprints were discovered in Chauvet cave in southern France and are thought to have been made by a young boy.

Chauvet cave, which was discovered in 1994, also contains 300 prehistoric wall paintings, considered the world's oldest. Radiocarbon datings of the paintings and camp-fire remains range from 23 000 to 32 000 years.

The footprints found at Laetoli in Tanzania are thought to belong to one of the better-known australopithecines, *A. afarensis*, and are estimated to be about 3,6 million years old. Left in wet volcanic ash baked hard by the sun, they are thought to be those of an adult male and a smaller hominid, possibly a female, who were accompanied by a younger companion, possibly a child.

New evidence emerges

A hominid skull unearthed in 2002 in the remote Djurab Desert in northern Chad has, however, caused scientists to reappraise their previously held beliefs about the point at which the family tree of our distant human ancestors diverged from that of apes. This skull, nicknamed Tourmai, which means 'hope of life' in the local Goran language of Chad, has a human-like face, but a braincase similar to that of a chimpanzee. The creature in question – more properly called *Sahelanthropus* – was about the size of a small chimp, probably lived on a diet consisting mainly of fruit, and may have walked on two legs. The most significant feature about this new 'find', however, is that Tourmai is about six to seven million years old. Prior to this discovery, the oldest hominid skull in existence dated back to about three million years ago.

Professor Michel Brunet, who was leading the team that made the find, described the event as a 'wonderful discovery'.

'This is the oldest hominid,' he is quoted as saying. 'It's seven million years old, so the divergence between chimp and human must be even older than we thought... The next skull we have is four million years later, so we don't know what happened in between. But with this new guy and species we have the beginnings of new knowledge. This is just the beginning of our knowledge of the human lineage.'[4]

In a similar vein, Professor Chris Stringer of the Natural History Museum in London, comments: 'This is the only relatively complete skull that has so far been discovered in the "fossil gap" of five million years between the ancestral apes of nine million years ago and the australopithecines of Africa, generally regarded as our close relatives, from four million years onwards...'[5]

Above Charles Darwin's *Origin of the Species* remains the cornerstone of modern evolutionary theory.

If the skull is a member of the family of man, maintains Professor Phillip Tobias, Witswatersrand University professor emeritus, '...it is the oldest claimant to being a hominid that's been discovered anywhere on the face of the planet. It makes us push back the time of origin of the human family further than we'd dreamt... We're getting nearer and nearer to the point of the great divide between ancient chimps and human ancestors. The nearer we get, the harder it's going to be to tell whether we're dealing with the earliest of the hominids or the last common ancestral population'.[6]

Chief Hintsa's skull

Despite the fact that the Great Fish River had been established as both the eastern border of Cape Colony and the boundary line between the colonists and the Xhosa, there was sustained pressure within the colony to expand eastwards and, by the mid-1830s, the colonial powers had turned their attention to the territory east of the Great Kei River: this was the country of the Gcaleka and was ruled over by chief Hintsa, who had established his Great Palace there.

And so it was that, in 1835, what had started out as sporadic incidents of resistance to colonial expansionism developed into a frontier war, when a number of Xhosa groups – most notably those led by Maqoma and Tyhali – crossed into the Cape and seized thousands of heads of cattle belonging to the colonists. These cattle they then drove back across the Great Kei River – Hintsa's country – for safekeeping, before taking refuge in the mountains, where they were safe from reprisal by British forces. In response, Sir Benjamin D'Urban led a force of British troops across the Great Kei for the first time on 15 April 1835. His main objective was to force Hintsa to return all the stolen cattle, but he also hoped to encourage the Gcaleka chief to support the British in their struggle against those Xhosa clans who had initiated the theft and who lived closer to the border.

Below Chief Hintsa, said to have been brutally murdered by the British, is still honoured as a fallen hero of the Gcaleka people.

Divide and conquer

To underscore his demands, D'Urban had offered British citizenship to the Mfengu clan – herdsmen to the Gcaleka and over whom the Gcaleka held hegemony – in return for the Mfengu's support against the Gcaleka. As a result, some Mfengu began to see the British as liberators and flocked to join their army. It was a classic strategy of divide and conquer and, having effectively instigated a rebellion within Hintsa's chiefdom, D'Urban de-clared war on the Gcaleka barely a week after crossing the Great Kei.

On 29 April, five days after war was declared, Hintsa, accompanied by a body of his men, visited the British military camp that had been established within his chiefdom. According to one account, he declared he would have come earlier, but had been 'dissuaded from it by some of his council, who said we should only kill him. He showed no appearance of fear.'[7]

Initially, the chief was treated with due deference and respect, though it appears the British authorities regarded him with some degree of condescension. As one settler put it: 'During the whole of the time, he has been overwhelmed with presents, at the same time that he was kept prisoner. Reminded one very much of the tickling of a trout.'[8]

The situation changed, however, when D'Urban received news that the Xhosa were massacring the Mfengu for their rebellious actions and he threatened to hang Hintsa unless he stopped the carnage. The Xhosa chief did as he was ordered, ending the bloodletting and effectively allowing the Mfengu to make off with over 20 000 Xhosa cattle. D'Urban also unarmed Hintsa and his retinue and increased the guard on his 'guest', and it thus became clear to all that Hintsa was no longer a favoured visitor, but merely a prisoner under guard.

As a result, when Hintsa was instructed to order the surrender of Maqoma and Tyhali, he sent secret messages to them, warning them that he was a prisoner and forbidding them to raise the ransom of 25 000 cattle and 500 horses for his release. He was then forced to accompany a column of British soldiers, led by Colonel (later, Sir) Harry Smith, to round up the cattle in question, and it was during this exercise – as the column marched along the banks of the Nqabara River – that Hintsa made his ill-fated break for freedom.

The chief is dead!

On or around 12 May 1835, Hintsa ka Phalo, chief of the Gcaleka and paramount chief of the Xhosa, was killed while attempting to escape from the British troops to whom he had, in effect, surrendered just a few days previously. Although details of Hintsa's actual killing remain sketchy, it seems he tried to gallop away from the column and down towards the river, but was pulled from his horse, possibly by Colonel Smith himself. He was then shot in the leg and the back as he continued to flee and collapsed into the water, where he was killed by one of his pursuers, George Southey, of the Corps of Guides, who delivered the *coup de grâce*, blowing the top of his head off in the process.

Hintsa's body was stripped of its jewellery and ornaments by British troops, two of whom cut off his ears for trophies, while others attempted to dig out his teeth with bayonets. His body was then left where it had fallen on the bank of the Nqabara River. His people later buried him nearby in an unmarked grave.

Some two years later, there was an official enquiry into Hintsa's death, but it threw little light on the actual circumstances of his killing – or the fact of his mutilation. During the evidence given by one R Daniels, for example, the following exchange took place:

'Did you see those ears?'

'I did see ears, but I do not know if they were Hintsa's.'

'In whose possession were those ears?'

'I cannot say, they were lying on the ground.'

'Were they shown as curiosities in the camp?'

'Not to me...'[9]

Enter Nicholas Gcaleka

With the passage of time, a belief arose that Hintsa had been beheaded immediately after death and that his head had been taken to Britain as a trophy. With his body buried in Africa and his head removed, claimed his supporters, his spirit, unable to rest, had been forced to wander in the wilderness ever since.

It was against this background, then, that 'Chief' Nicholas Tilana Gcaleka, replete with dreadlocks, leopard-skin attire and staff, burst onto the scene in 1996 to announce to an astonished world, including the Xhosa themselves, that he had been visited by his ancestors in a dream and that they had instructed him to fetch Chief Hintsa's head from Scotland and return it to Africa.

Did you know?

The skull of Chief Hintsa, a Xhosa paramount chief killed by British soldiers over 160 years ago, was alleged to have been found in a forest in Scotland in 1996.

Despite the fact that senior Xhosa chiefs had distanced themselves from both Gcaleka and his self-proclaimed quest, and that the British High Commissioner to South Africa had stated during Queen Elizabeth II's official visit to South African in 1995 that British officials had no idea where the head was, nor if it had ever been brought to the United Kingdom, the flamboyant 'Chief' Nicholas arrived at Heathrow airport on 15 February 1996 to considerable fanfare...

London's *Daily Telegraph* of 16 February 1996 was one of the first to report the arrival of the erstwhile chief:

'South Africa's leading witchdoctor [sic] arrived in Britain yesterday to search for the severed head of his ancestor and bring peace to his homeland. Dressed in a leopard skin, red skirt and a bright red cloak, Nicholas Tilana Gcaleka flew into Heathrow from Johannesburg carrying a fly-whisk and a short spear wrapped in airport security tape. Chief Gcaleka launched into a rhythmic chant at the arrivals lounge to conjure up the spirits which, he says, will help him in his quest to find the head of his great-great-uncle.

The head he seeks belongs to Chief Hintsa, Chief of the Xhosa nation, who was killed 160 years ago in the Eastern Cape at the start of the Sixth Frontier War by George Southey, a military guide to a British expedition. The king's body was left for his own people to find, but legend has it that when they did, the head was missing.

'Chief Gcaleka believes that the king's head was brought to Britain and he says that the spirits have told him that it is to be found in Scotland. He also believes that many of South Africa's problems have been caused by King Hinta's headless spirit wandering the country. Chief Gcaleka hopes that if he can reunite the head with the body his country's troubles will be over.

'British historians and museums have offered to help him but say that they can find no trace of the king's head.

'"I am going to search with the spirits," Chief Gcaleka, South Africa's most famous *sangoma* or spiritual healer, said yesterday: "It is here – I have no doubt about it. I know where it is" – although he refused to say where.

'Emerging from the customs hall, he astonished fellow travellers by chanting and then loudly announcing the reason for his visit.

'"We are here for the remains of King Hintsa, who was beheaded by British troops on 12 May 1835, by the order of Sir Henry Smith," he yelled across the arrivals lounge. "He was the king of the Xhosa nation.

'"On 12 May 1835, Sir Henry Smith took the throne from King Hintsa. We have no king for 161 years. By coming here, we are bringing our king back to South Africa. President Nelson Mandela is with us all the time."

'Asked how he hoped to find the missing head, Chief Gcaleka said: "I am going to search with the spirits. I am coming here on a spiritual search for the head of King Hintsa."

'He refused to answer any more questions and his spokesman, Robert Pringle, said: "He is a great witchdoctor and, in the tradition of great South African witchdoctors, he is not going to give away anything for nothing. If you want him to speak English, you have got to pay him, basically."

'The chief was then led away with a police escort before climbing into the back of a stretched Cadillac limousine. His itinerary over the next two weeks is said to depend on the will of the spirits, but he is expected to start his search at the Natural History Museum in London before travelling to Fort George, near Inverness, the headquarters of the long-disbanded 72nd and 75th Highland Regiments, which fought in the campaign in which the king died.'

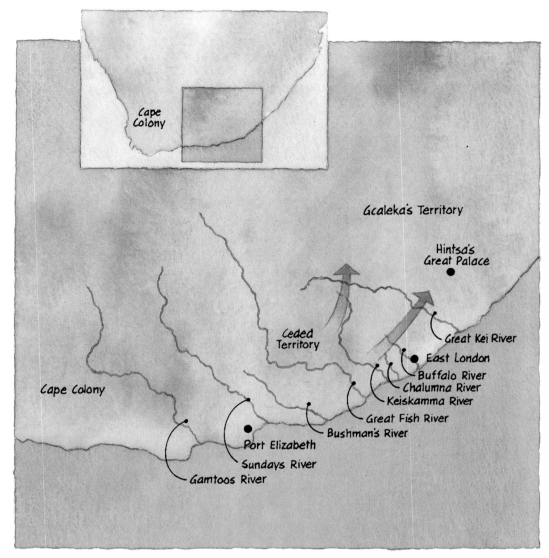

Gcaleka's quest

After spending two weeks in the United Kingdom, 'Chief' Gcaleka revealed that he had found Chief Hintsa's' skull in a forest near to a white pony, exactly as his ancestors had predicted. He then returned to South Africa and held a press conference. He displayed the skull he had 'found' and pointed to a defect on the side of the skull, which he declared, was the place where Hintsa had been struck by the fatal bullet.

But Gcaleka's claims met with considerable resistance. Xhosa traditional leaders disagreed with his findings, claiming that Hintsa's skull had disintegrated when he was shot, and the Xhosa royal family accused him of being a fake. Shortly afterwards, the skull Gcaleka had brought back from Scotland was confiscated by local police and sent for scientific analysis to the University of Cape Town.

The investigating team that had been set up to examine the skull consisted of Professor Deon Knobel, as coordinator, Dr Graham Louw of UCT's Department of Anatomy and Cell Biology; Professor Vincent Phillips of Stellenbosch University's Oral and Dental Teaching

Hospital, and Professor Phillip Tobias of the Palaeo-anthropology Research Unit in the University of the Witwatersrand's Department of Anatomy and Human Biology.

The team subsequently revealed its findings at the 27th Annual Congress of the Anatomical Society of Cape Town. They concluded that the skull was not that of a male of unmixed African origin, and indications were that it belonged to a middle-aged woman, probably of European descent. They also pointed out that the 'bullet hole' pointed out to the press by Gcaleka at his news conference had none of the characteristic radial fracture lines or inward bevelling one would normally associate with a bullet wound. Nor was there an exit wound or exit damage of any sort.

In conclusion, the investigating team stated that: '...[the] cranium is not that of King Hintsa, who at death would have been an adult male of about 46 years of age, or unmixed African origin.'[10]

Not unexpectedly, of course, Gcaleka disputed this finding. Not only did he claim that the skull he had brought back from Scotland was not the same one the scientists had produced – despite the fact that the skull in question proved to be identical in every way to the one he had revealed at the press conference – but he also questioned whether scientists were qualified to deliberate on a spiritual matter of this nature since they '[did] not dream' the way he did.

Refusing to accept the findings of the investigative panel, Gcaleka declared that he was 'not listening to those experts, who are of European origin themselves', and demanded that he be given the skull back so that it could be given a proper burial. Not surprisingly, his demand was denied.

Facing fraud

In a final twist in this amazing tale, days after scientists had announced that the skull Gcaleka had brought back from Scotland was a fake, the supposed 'chief' was arrested on fraud charges in the Eastern Cape and was consequently held in custody after it was established that he was unable to raise bail money of R3000. The charges related to the issuing of cheques allegedly signed by Gcaleka – whose real name, it was now revealed, was Nicholas Mbambatho – when buying liquor and groceries from a store in 1991 and from the Gilbey's liquor company in 1992. His second appearance in court in December 1997 was thus duly reported upon the by the East London's *Daily Despatch* on 13 December 1997:

'Chief Nicholas Gcaleka, whose claim to fame was a hunt for a chief's skull, was denied bail and remanded in custody in the Durban regional court yesterday. Chief Gcaleka, otherwise known as Mr Nicholas Mbambatho, 45, is facing a charge of fraud involving more than R140 000. He allegedly bought liquor with a stolen cheque.

'The public prosecutor, Ms P Pillay, urged the magistrate, Mr A Hofert, not to grant Mr Mbambatho bail at this stage because the accused had been evading police since 1991, which made it difficult for police to conclude their investigation.

'Mr Mbambatho was remanded in custody until 7 January next year to enable police to complete their investigations.'

According to the article, Chief Gcaleka was taken to Westville prison in his 'traditional regalia'.

A skull's story

While the true story of Hintsa's skull remains unsure, and the lack of physical evidence means that neither claim – that the head had been removed or that it had disintegrated over time – can be refuted with any certainty, the skull of the middle-aged woman Gcaleka had apparently unearthed in Scotland has indeed found a new 'resting' place. Under South Africa's Human Tissue Act, the private possession of human body parts or skeletal remains is forbidden, and the skull is currently housed in UCT's forensic medicine department, where it is used solely for academic purposes.

Sarah Bartmann – the Hottentot Venus

Sarah Bartmann – or Saartjie Baartmann, as she was known for nearly 200 years – was a Khoi woman who was born in the Gamtoos Valley in what is now the Eastern Cape in 1789. She later moved to the Cape and it was here that she met a ship's surgeon who persuaded her that she could earn a fortune by displaying her distinct 'Hottentot' features in public. And so it was that in 1810 the 21-year-old Sarah Bartmann set sail for foreign shores.

In England, where she was regarded as somewhat of a curiosity and a freak, she toured the country with fairs and travelling shows under the name of the 'Hottentot Venus'. The main fascination for the thousands of people who flocked to see her were her large buttocks and – for the scientific community of the time – her genitalia, which were thought to include exceptionally long labia, hanging down to form what scientists called the 'Hottentot apron' or 'tablier' – or, alternatively, the 'curtain of shame'.

When she wasn't featuring in any of the outlandish shows, she was displayed like a wild beast in a cage. In fact, it was during one such exhibition in Piccadilly, London, that abolitionists of the African Institution raised in the press the question of her freedom. As a result of this, she was formally questioned about both her actions and her relationship with her exhibitor and, during the interview, dismissed any suggestion that she had either been brought to England against her will, or that she was being coerced to perform. She made it quite clear that she had left Africa of her own free will, and that she was more than happy with her current situation. As Sarah Bartmann herself pointed out, she was receiving half the proceeds from her act and this enabled her to employ two servants of her own. The reason why she acted out the role of a wild beast at times was simply because it was part of the show, she explained.

In 1815, a French entrepreneur took her to Paris, where – despite reported protestations that she was perfectly happy with her lot – she fell victim to alcoholism and prostitution. It was here, too, that she was lent out to physicians and scientists for examination when not on display, and in March of that year she was examined 'in the interests of science' by a number of France's leading experts and a nude portrait of her was drawn. She died of an 'inflammatory and eruptive malady' in Paris on 29 December 1815, at the age of 26 years.

Life after death

Given the morbid curiosity surrounding people of Khoi origin among apparently 'learned' Europeans, it is not surprising that, 'in the interests of science', it was decided to dissect Bartmann's corpse after her

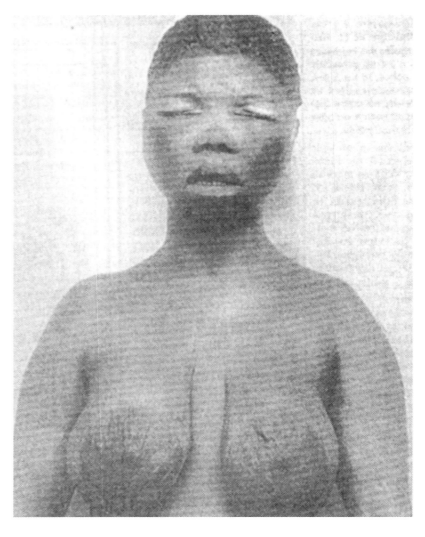

Below After her death Sarah Bartmann's body was preserved 'in the interests of science'. Her 'death mask', a wax cast of her body, was made by Baron Georges Cuvier in 1816.

death. This task was given to the leading French anatomist of the day, Baron Georges Cuvier (1769-1832), who was Chancellor of the University of Paris. Cuvier and is generally regarded as the founder of palaeontology and comparative anatomy, first had Bartmann's body cast in wax and then dissected her, paying particular attention to her genitals, which, along with her brain, were removed and preserved in glass jars. Having completed his study, Bartmann's skeleton was then reassembled.

In 1824, Cuvier published a scientific paper on his findings and included a colour portrait as an illustration of type. Following on from this, her genitalia and brain then went on display at the Musée de l'Homme (Museum of Mankind) in Paris. (These exhibits were only withdrawn from public view in 1974, although she was further displayed at the Musée d'Orsay in May 1994 in an exhibition entitled *La sculpture ethnographique de la Vénus hottentote à la Tehura de Gauguin*.)

Sarah Bartmann comes home

On 14 December 1995, Cecil le Fleur, speaking on behalf of the Griqua people, addressed the South African parliament, asking them to intervene in order to obtain the return of the plaster cast, skeletal and other remains of Sarah Bartmann from the French government. But it was only after a long period of intense negotiation and the passing by the French of a carefully worded law on 6 March 2002 designed to prevent this being used as a precedent in other cases, the French government finally handed over Bartmann's remains to the South African government. The official handing-over ceremony took place at the South African Embassy in Paris on 29 April 2002.

'France wants to restore the dignity of Saartje Bartmann, who was humiliated as a woman and exploited as an African,' said French Research Minister Roger-Gérard Schwartzenberg.

'Saartjie Bartmann is beginning her final journey home, to a free, democratic, non-sexist and non-racist South Africa. She's a symbol of our national need to confront our past and restore dignity to all our people,' responded Ambassador Thuthukile Skweyiya.

Bartmann's remains were then flown back to South Africa, where they arrived in Cape Town on the morning of Friday, 3 May 2002, to much fanfare.

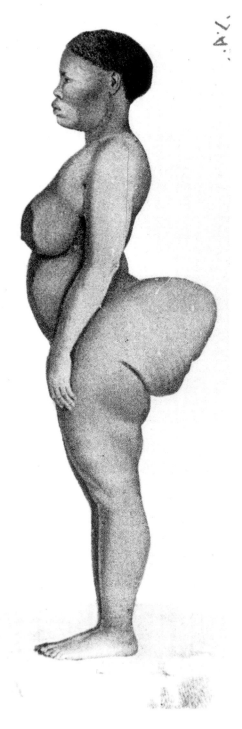

Right Sarah's distinct features, particularly her protruding buttocks, were so foreign to even learned and 'enlightened' Europeans that they attracted intense interest on the continent.

Did you know?

After being exhibited as a freak of nature in a Paris museum for almost two centuries, the remains of Sarah (Saartjie) Bartmann were finally returned to South Africa soil in 2002.

Present at a ceremony held at the airport to welcome her back to the continent she had left almost two centuries before was a host of dignitaries, including Arts and Culture Deputy Minister Bridgitte Mabandla and Western Cape Premier at the time Peter Marais.

'The return of Saartjie Bartmann is going to give rise to the rediscovery of the pride of the Khoisan people,' Marais told an emotionally charged ceremony.

A box containing Bartmann's remains, draped in a South African flag and flanked by six Khoisan children, was wheeled into the airport, after which it was transported to the mortuary of 2 Military Hospital in Wynberg where it was kept for burial.

The remains of Sarah (Saartjie) Bartmann were finally laid to rest on the banks of the Gamtoos River, near Hankey in the Eastern Cape, on Women's Day, Friday, 9 August 2002. Perhaps a fitting conclusion to the story of Sarah Bartmann are the words of researcher and writer Gail Smith in an article published in *The Star* entitled 'Why we froth about Saartjie':

'The story of Bartmann is about the hidden history of South Africa... Her historic repatriation, a first in the history of France, is thanks largely to the women of colour in South Africa and from around the globe who have dedicated years of research, writing poetry and plays to honour Bartmann's legacy and to reclaim her from the clutches of racism.'[11]

'In the interests of science...'

During the 18th and 19th centuries, the sciences of genetics, biochemistry and physiology were unknown and the study of anatomy was the chief method by which anthropologists made 'objective contributions' to the advancement of knowledge. Often, however, the point of the exercise was to 'prove' the superiority of the white race, but for such 'contributions' to have validity, it was important to work with a 'pure' example of type. As Bartmann was believed to fall into this category, there was much excitement within the European scientific community to 'learn' as much as possible from her. More accurately, 'experiments' of this nature were usually used to support the grotesque stereotypes about Africans and African sexuality circulating at the time. But Bartmann was not the only member of her race to suffer indignity as a scientific curiosity.

In 1860, two young San children – a boy and a girl – were shipped from their home somewhere along the Orange River to England.[12] According to *Trophy Skulls, Museums and the San* by Alan G Morris '...The boy died within a few years of his arrival in England, but the girl lived until June 1864, dying at the age of about 22 years. Her body was sent to the Royal College of Surgeons, where it was dissected by the English comparative and human anatomists W H Flower and J Murie (1867). Her skeleton was kept and, although many of the bones were destroyed during the bombing of the College in World War II, the remains that have survived now reside in the British Museum of Natural History'.[13]

Morris also describes how a similar fate befell a third 'bushwoman' known as Keri Keri, who, having died of septic pneumonia in Oudtshoorn, Cape Province, in 1939, was transported to the University of Witwatersrand's Department of Anatomy for dissection.[14]

A morbid curiosity

The so-called Hottentot race had long fascinated European scientists. Khoikhoi males, for example, were believed by some to be monorchids, meaning they had only one testicle, and females, with their tablier, it was speculated, were creatures of unbridled lust. (Europe's learned men of science were fascinated with Bartmann's vagina because it was assumed that Hottentot women had genitals so different from 'ordinary' humans as to make them part of the animal kingdom.) In other words, so-called Hottentots were regarded at best as noble savages and, at worst, as little better than animals. The Swedish naturalist and physician, Carolus Linnaeus (1707–78), for example, classified Hottentots as *Homo monstrosus monorchides*, whom, he maintained occupied a side branch on the tree of human evolution.[15]

The origin of the myth regarding Khoisan males may have been the writings of Jean-Baptiste Tavernier, who visited the Cape in 1649 and later wrote, '...Both men and women are lean and short of stature; and as soon as a male child is born, the mother cuts away his right testicle, and gives him sea water to drink and tobacco to chew. This right testicle is removed since they say it makes him speedier in running: some among them can overtake roebucks...'.

Trial by water:
The heroes of West Driefontein

It all began at around 9.30 am on Saturday, 26 October 1968. Two hours earlier, 1200 men had made their way below ground to begin another shift and everything appeared to be functioning normally. At the time, the West Driefontein Mine had been in production for just over 16 years, and arguably the best-equipped gold mine in the world – and certainly the most profitable.

The first hint of trouble occurred when the banksman – who signals to the hoist operator to which level a man cage or a rock skip must be sent – received a message from the Onsetter – his assistant stationed at one of the levels below ground – in Number 4 Shaft that 'a great deal of water' was pouring down the mine shaft.

Water, water everywhere…

The West Driefontein mine is built on a bank of dolomite rock that extends from about 600 metres to about 1200 metres below ground. Over millions of years, this layer of rock has been eroded by water falling on the surface of the ground and has created 'pockets' of water inside the rock. In other words, this dolomite layer is rather like a massive sponge and

Below A natural 'leak' in the Driefontein gold mine. *Bottom right* A typical drive in the mine, which would have been similar to that around which the crisis occurred.

contains thousands of small water reservoirs or 'pockets'. When one of these 'pockets' is breached – whether by mining operations or from other causes – the water flows out and makes its way down through the rock to its next natural collection point.

It is well to remember, however, that when a 'leak' occurs at the depth where most gold mining actually takes place, there is likely to be over 1000 metres of standing water overhead, which means that escaping water does so under tremendous pressure.

Some water 'pockets' are small and some large. The largest of these are referred to as 'compartments' and have been given names. Blyvooruitzicht Mine, Western Deep Levels and the greater portion of West Driefontein, for example, lie either under or adjacent to the Oberholzer Compartment and the Number 4 Shaft in West Driefontein is located near to the Bank Compartment, which is thought to be around 100 square kilometres in size and holds about 400 000 million litres of water.

Getting the water out

Getting excess water out of West Driefontein gold mine was a standard daily task. In the early days, for example, about 25 million litres of water a day were lifted out of the mine. This capacity was increased to 110 million litres a day in the early 1960s and then doubled to 250 million litres a day when mining operations moved under the Bank Compartment and through a particularly large fault in a rock universally referred to as 'Big Boy'. Watertight doors had also been installed to protect the pumping shafts up to Level 16.

Water in a mine is not pumped from the bottom of the mine to the top, but is lifted out in relays. A pump station 2000 metres underground, for example, will lift the water about 1000 metres, where another 'relay' pump will lift it the rest of the distance to the surface.

In the case of the Number 4 Shaft, which was nearest to the 'leak', there was only one small pump chamber at $13^{3}/_{4}$ Level. All the other pump chambers serviced Shafts 1, 2, 3 and 5. This meant there was no system for getting water out of the bottom of Number 4 Shaft below Level $13^{3}/_{4}$.

Mines such as Driefontein also have a sophisticated drainage system. Large drains run alongside the drives – horizontal passages – and carry water from the extremities of the mine to the mine shaft. In the case of Number 4 Shaft, water draining to the shaft was rerouted along drainpipes to Number 3 Shaft, where it was lifted to the surface by a series of relay pumps.

The precise circumstances surrounding the events of that sunny Saturday morning in 1968 remain uncertain – the most likely explanation is that there was a small earth tremor the night before, but for some reason a breach occurred somewhere between Levels 4 and 6 and, although no one realised it at the time, millions of litres of water had begun flooding into the mine.

Trying to hold back the flood

The banksman who had received the message about the 'great deal of water' flooding into the Number 4 Shaft immediately contacted the General Manager's office, where he spoke to LR Alexander, the Underground Manager on duty that morning. Alexander decided to investigate the matter personally and, accompanied by Jack Cuthbertson, a mine overseer, went down into the mine to have a look for himself.

The truth is that the two men were not unduly worried at first because 'leaks' involving 'a great deal of water' occurred all the time and the mine was accustomed to fixing them. Also, what sometimes happened in a situation such as this was that there would be a great inrush of water into the mine when the 'pocket' was first breached, then the flow would diminish as it ran dry. With this reassuring knowledge at the back of their minds, the two men got in the lift cage and descended into the mine.

Did you know?

In 1968, the quick thinking and brave decisions of a handful of individuals saved the West Driefontein gold mine (now Driefontein Goldfields) from being completely flooded and shut down for good.

Meanwhile, news that a 'leak' had occurred had also reached the the office of Harry Wheeler, a sectional manager on duty.

'That's a piece of cake,' he remarked. 'We'll have that fixed in half an hour.'

It was a comment he was not likely to forget.

When Alexander and Cuthbertson descended below Level 4, the sight and sound that greeted them was beyond their wildest imaginings. The 'great deal of water' in question was a veritable torrent, half a metre deep. It was pouring out of one of the side passages, into the Number 4 Shaft and then cascading to the bottom of the lift shaft 1200 metres below, carrying with it lengths of timber and other assorted flotsam. And when the two men tried to descend below Level 6, the water pounded on the roof of the lift cage with such force and volume it caused the cage to yo-yo dangerously.

The information Alexander and Cuthbertson had first received said that the flow of water into the mine shaft was about 10 centimetres deep, but this was clearly no longer the case. In fact, the volume of water flooding into the mine seemed to have increased dramatically. Not only were the drains completely inadequate for this volume of water, but the bottom of the mine shaft was already flooded and the water level was rising.

This was clearly a serious situation, but no one at the time realised just how serious. This wasn't just a routine 'leak' involving a fairly large pocket of water trapped in the rock: somewhere between Levels 4 and 6, a breach into the Bank Compartment had occurred. Nearly 400 million litres of water a day were now pouring into the workings.

Below Once operations have been completed in certain parts of the mines, drives such as this one on Level 12 of the Driefontein gold mine are abandoned.

Everyone out!

At 10.10 am, Harry Wheeler also went into the mine to evaluate the situation at first hand.

'I went to 6 Level where the water had formed a stream three feet (1 metre) deep rushing down the shaft,' he said. 'I realised that the shaft would be out of commission below Level 6 and that we'd better start evacuating the men.

'Then I tried to walk in on Level 6 against this fast flowing stream. When I got to the ventilation door, the rush of air was so strong that I just couldn't get through the door. And so I came back, went up to the surface and reported to the manager that the water was much more than any of us had expected and that we had already sent messages down to the men to make their way to Number 3 Shaft.[16]

Shift bosses had been sent down into the mine to relay instructions to the men. The miners were to leave their stations and make their way back to the surface – not via Number 4 Shaft, which had been declared out of commission below Level 6, but by 'legging it' to the Number 3 Shaft, a three-kilometre walk in knee-deep water!

The evacuation went smoothly and by 5.30 pm all the miners were out of the mine – except two, that is: Alberto Noife and Luiz Sandela were trapped in a small pump chamber on 13¾ Level, Number 4 Shaft. This underground chamber, which was about the size of a large room, was filled with pumping equipment, and could only be reached using the hoist in the Number 4 Shaft, but this lift shaft was no longer operational below Level 6. Unless a way could be found to rescue the two men, they were certain to drown.

Luiz Sandela explains what happened...

'We really did not know what was happening on that day when all that water came pouring down the shaft, except that there was a big noise. At first, we had the telephone and we tried to reach the [Team Leaders] at the bottom of the shaft, but there was no one there. Then we rang the banksman and he said to stay where we were till the cage came to get us. We waited, but no cage came. Then the lights went out. Then the telephone was no good and still the water was coming down. When the lights were gone, we used one of the lights on our hats and kept the other one for later. We were very frightened. It was cold and we thought we were going to die. Much time went by and no one came for us. We climbed up on the set and sat there...[17]

Wet and shivering, the two men cowered in the dark while a solid wall of water poured past the entrance to the pump chamber. Second by second, the hours slowly ticked by. But the two men had not been forgotten, and frantic efforts were under way to launch a rescue operation. The problem was how to reach them...

Operation rescue

It had been estimated that the two miners had about 12 hours before the water filling up the mine reached the pump chamber where they were trapped. The problem was that the signal bells, indicating to the hoist driver to which level he should raise or lower the cage, were out in the Number 4 Shaft. Also, the force of water crashing down the lift shaft made lowering a man cage extremely dangerous. Not only would the cascading water cause the lift cage to yo-yo unpredictably, but the deafening noise meant that communication of any sort was virtually impossible. What was more, the only way a rescue attempt had any chance of success was if the cage sent down to bring them out, stopped precisely opposite their station.

It was also important not to endanger the lives of any other miners through a futile or ill-planned rescue attempt. If the calculations about the depth of water in the mine shaft were wrong, for example, there was a danger that a cage lowered to rescue the two miners might be submerged, drowning the rescuers.

To solve this dilemma, overseer Jack Cuthbertson came up with a truly brilliant improvisation. First a sloping canopy, like the roof of a house, would be built over the cage to deflect the water pouring down the shaft, then a polythene ball on a rod was fixed inside the cage. This was to act like the ball cock inside a toilet cistern: If the cage went under water, it would force the ball up the rod and this would be apparent when the cage was brought back to the surface.

The trial run proved successful – although the cage yo-yoed inside the shaft, it descended as low as the pump chamber, without going underwater – but the next problem was communication.

'When the bells went, we got walkie-talkie equipment, this is two-way radio,' Cuthbertson explained. 'I still had a telephone line open from the engine driver on the hoist as far as Level 4 [above the point where the water was flowing in]. Then I had to two-way communication with the men in the cage.

'In the cage, you couldn't see or hear anything because of the noise of falling water, so they had to be told they'd arrived at their destination and get out. They then had to step blind from a cage that was yo-yoing as much as three feet and hope for the best – though, of course, once they were through the curtain of water, they could see what they were doing.

'We had also fitted big lights, loco lights, to the cage in the hope that the men in the pump chamber would see these and jump into the cage, but the cascade of water down there was so solid that they did not see them.'[18]

An act of extreme bravery

Two men, shaft timberman W C Theron and team leader Vascoe then volunteered to go down and make the rescue. The man cage would be lowered to Level 133/4, where it would remain for a maximum of three minutes before being raised again.

And so down they went, descending below the waterfall pouring down the shaft. When the cage finally came to a halt, both men jumped out and landed in the pump chamber – and there they were: Noife and Sandela were sitting on top of some equipment perched up under the roof – naked in anticipation of having to swim for it when the water reached the pump chamber.

The men were cold and scared, but unharmed.

'When the cage came, we saw no lights and could hear nothing until, suddenly, the boss boy came with a rope and they pulled us through the water. But we were very, very happy when we got to the top,' said Sandela.[19]

All's well that ends well

The rescued men reached the surface at 7.20, having been underground for 12 hours.

Vascoe later described the rescue:

'At 6.30, Mr Cuthbertson told me that two pump boys had been left underground at Level $13^3/_4$, and he asked me if I was prepared to go down with Mr Theron to fetch them. I replied that I would. He asked me if I was not afraid and I replied that I was not. On the surface, I had not been afraid, but I must admit that when I saw the amount of water and the noise it was making, I was afraid, but something [had to] be done to save the pump boys.

'When the cage stopped, Mr Theron was informed through the walkie-talkie that we were at Level $13^3/_4$. We could not see the station, as the water was pouring down past the cage. I left the cage station, and went to find the pump boys. They had removed their boots and hard hats, and they were very scared. I made them put their boots and hard hats on and we returned to the station. They were afraid to climb through the water into the cage, so I

Opposite A cross-section of East Driefontein, similar to that of West Driefontein where the miners were trapped, reflects the various levels and underground infrastructure of gold mines.

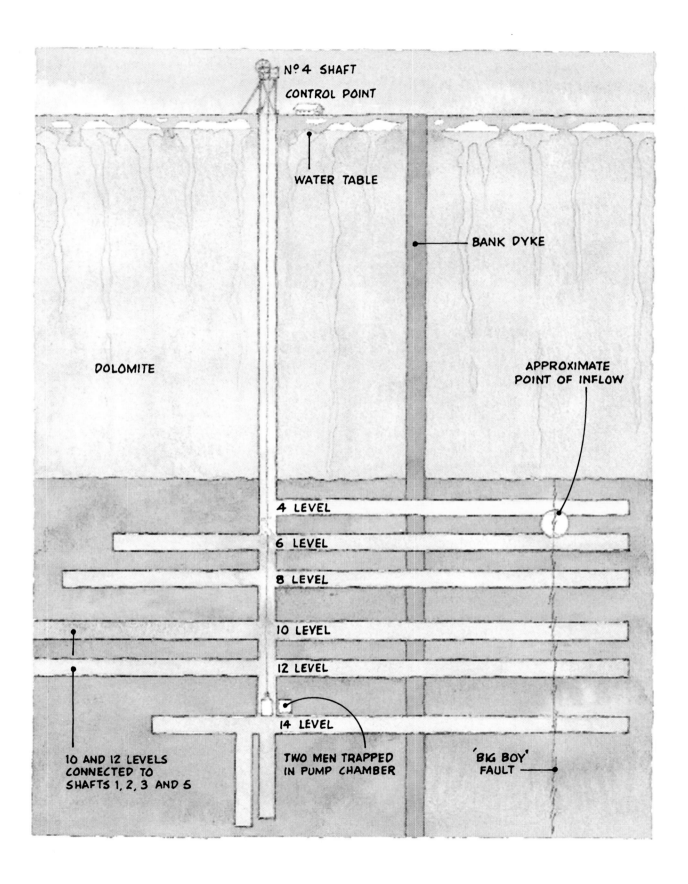

N° 4 SHAFT

CONTROL POINT

WATER TABLE

BANK DYKE

DOLOMITE

APPROXIMATE
POINT OF INFLOW

4 LEVEL

6 LEVEL

8 LEVEL

10 LEVEL

12 LEVEL

14 LEVEL

10 AND 12 LEVELS
CONNECTED TO
SHAFTS 1, 2, 3 AND 5

TWO MEN TRAPPED
IN PUMP CHAMBER

'BIG BOY'
FAULT

climbed back into the cage, collected the rope and climbed back onto the station again. I tied the rope to the first man and while Mr Theron held the rope, I made him climb through the water into the cage. I did the same with the second man and I then returned to the cage and we were pulled to the surface.'[20]

As Underground Manager, L R Alexander would later remark, 'Looking back now on the evacuation of these men from the working places through water that was running very strongly by then, it seems to me close to a miracle that we managed to get them out without a single loss. This I think was one of the most amazing and outstanding achievements of the whole operation.'[21]

The Chamber of Mines of South Africa awarded its Bronze Medal for Outstanding Bravery – known as 'the miner's VC [Victoria Cross]' – to Vascoe and Theron for their bravery.

Saving the mine

By early evening all those in danger below ground had been removed from the mine. Now management could concentrate on sealing off the leak, which because the shafts were all connected was now causing flooding the other shafts, thereby threatening the entire mine.

The command centre initially set up by General Manager Ray Buley – who had actually expected the situation to be resolved in a couple of days – would, in fact, remain operational 24 hours a day for the next 17 days: a time of truly monumental effort by management and workforce alike.

There were always at least three senior managers on duty, and constant communication was maintained with the men working below ground. The managers would make decisions on the spot, and this was one of the main reasons why the mine was able to survive the crisis.

Early estimates on the volume of water flooding the mines were wholly inaccurate, and the situation was desperate. And so it was that on Sunday, 27 October, Adriaan Louw, chairman of the West Driefontein company and of Gold Fields South Africa issued a statement in which he estimated that 40 million gallons [150 million litres] of water were entering the mine, but it took days before revised estimates suggested that upwards of 100 million gallons [385 million litres] per day were flooding the mine.

It had been realised at the beginning of the crisis that it would be necessary to 'plug' one or more of the drives in order to halt the flooding, but in practice this is both difficult and dangerous, especially in situations where the plugs are constructed in desperate circumstances. The first attempt to plug one of the drives was made on Level 12, but the workings were flooded before the plug could be completed and the attempt failed. That, however, was just the first of many setbacks...

GOLD MINES – ACCIDENT DATA 1984–2001*

Year	Fatalities	Fatality Rate*	Injuries	Injury Rate*
1984	588	1,23	13 611	28,49
1985	540	1,13	13 107	27,31
1986	709	1,46	11 515	23,67
1987	547	1,15	9969	20,93
1988	509	1,09	8828	18,86
1989	557	1,24	9034	20,08
1990	531	1,25	8183	19,21
1991	461	1,21	7531	19,80
1992	407	1,13	7587	21,04
1993	426	1,23	7368	21,34
1994	371	1,08	6888	20,00
1995	415	1,27	6243	19,13
1996	315	1,04	5909	19,56
1997	277	0,95	5707	19,53
1998	252	1,08	4648	19,87
1999	207	0,98	4202	19,90
2000	173	0,91	3549	18,62
#2001	192	1,05	3372	18,36

* Rates = /1000 persons at work
# = provisional

All sorts of difficulties were emerging.

Another problem was that the water in the Level 12 drive began had begun to pour into the Number 3 sub-vertical shaft, cascading to the bottom of the mine and drawing air from the shaft after it. This resulted in a partial vacuum on Level 12, causing extremely strong winds to occur, some as high as 200 kilometre per hour.

Suddenly, the men on the Level 12 drive – who had been trying to construct the first plug and, who having failed, were on their way back to Number 3 Shaft where they would be brought to the surface – found themselves trapped in the middle of a powerful whirlwind and were forced to take shelter against the walls for their own safety. And it was only after many hours that they managed to get to a small lift operating between levels 10 and 12 and were able to get out that way. In fact, when one of the miners who had been trapped reached the surface, he walked out and has never been seen since.

It was soon realised, however, that despite the enormous difficulties involved, the only answer was to plug the main drives on levels 10 and 12, and on 5 November, the chairman announced at a press conference that engineers were attempting to install plugs on each of the levels connecting to Number 4 Shaft. The process, he added somewhat despondently, was expected to take as long as four weeks. He thus concluded that, '...on the presently available figures of storage, pumping capacity and the rate of inflow, this effort will unfortunately not succeed.'[22] What he was, in effect, saying was that the mine was in imminent danger of being completely swamped by the water and that there was nothing anyone could do about it.

Underground, meanwhile, work was continuing. Not only did all the equipment and materials have to be manhandled into place, but the miners themselves were working in extremely confined spaces, as often as not in water up to their waists. But everyone worked unbelievably hard, not just until the end of a shift, but until a particular job was done, some individuals even staying at their posts for 48 hours at a stretch.

While the plugs were being installed in the Level 10 and 12 drives, the water level in the mine continued to increase and even though more and more pumps were brought in, the only effect they had was to slow down the rate at which the mine was filling up.

On 12 November, while the sixth pump on Level 20 was being repaired, the motor in the seventh pump burned out. Five pumps alone clearly were not sufficient and the water rose to five centimetres from the top of the dam wall before the sixth pump was repaired. It was estimated that if another 10 minutes had elapsed without the sixth pump coming on line, the entire pump chamber would have been swamped. And since this pump chamber was at the very heart of the effort to pump water out of the mine, if it had gone down, then the mine would have almost certainly gone down with it. West Driefontein mine was saved from disaster literally at the last minute and, in order to achieve this feat, workers at the mine had completed in 17 days work that under normal circumstances would have taken three to four months.

AP Cartwright, the author who documented the entire episode on behalf of West Driefontein, later wrote that, in all the long history of mining, '... there has never been a finer story than this. It is a wonderful record of courage, endurance and great engineering skill.'[23] His words are indeed a fitting epitaph to one of the greatest achievements against seemingly insurmountable odds in the history of South African mining.

Danger ahead!

There are 52 gold mines in South Africa, not all of which are operational all the time. These gold mines employ about 183 000 people and the mining industry as a whole around 383 000. Kloof is the largest gold mine in the country, employing around 18 000 people with the Agnes, the smallest, employing only 180. South Africa produces around 17 per cent of the world's supply of gold, but how safe are our mines?

This is, in effect, a rather difficult question to answer. Mining by its very nature is a dangerous occupation, and responses to this question tend to be somewhat subjective. South Africa's safety record in its metaliferrous mines – iron ore, bauxite, etc. – compare favourably with those overseas. (This is mainly because the underground labour employed in these mines is relatively small.) Our coal mines also compare very well, but there is no direct comparison with overseas gold mines.

The Lemba:
The 'black Jews' of South Africa

The Lemba – who number approximately 70 000 – are an Nguni-speaking people who are found predominantly in Limpopo Province but, according to Lemba oral tradition, their ancient Jewish ancestors migrated to southern Africa from Judea 2–3000 years ago.

Until recently, thei Lemba claim to Jewish ancestry was treated with some scepticism by traditional Jewish authorities, but recent genetic tests carried out in both the United Kingdom and South Africa have confirmed that Lemba males, particularly those from the Buba clan, display an unusually high incidence of a particular Y-chromosome haplotype, referred to as the Cohen Modal Haplotype (CMH), which is commonly found among Sephardi and Ashkenazi Jews. Although the CMH is also found in other Middle Eastern populations and is not restricted to people of Jewish extraction, DNA testing has indicated that 45 per cent of Ashkenazi priests and 56 per cent of Sephardic priests have the same CMH genetic signature. In fact, scientists have also established that the incidence of this chromosome among Lemba men is about 8,8 per cent – similar to that found among Jewish men in general – and that the incidence of this haplotype among the Buba clan specifically is in the region of 53 per cent.

From Jerusalem to Johannesburg

Over the centuries, certain black communities in western, central and southern Africa have claimed strong Jewish links dating back to biblical times and, although there is indeed historical and anthropological evidence to support these claims, until recently there has been no verifiable genetic proof.

The presence of Jewish communities outside of the Middle East and dating back thousands of years has been well documented. A Jewish presence in Egypt and North Africa, for example, was described in the Book of Exodus, and during the 10th and 9th centuries BC, both King David and King Solomon adopted expansionist policies that sought to expand Jewish influence across the Mediterranean, into North Africa, through the Horn of Africa and into Persia. Also, regional conflicts, such as the Assyrian attack on Israel in the 8th century BC and the Babylonian invasion of Jerusalem 200 years later, drove many Jews away from their homeland and into exile. So it is against this background of turmoil and transition, that numerous Jewish settlements were established throughout the region, as far south as the fringes of the Sahara and along the east coast of Africa.

According to Dr Rudo Mathivha, the Lemba's Jewish ancestry dates back about 2500 years when a group of Jews, led by the house of Buba, left Judea and settled in the Yemen. This original move, it is thought, was made to establish some kind of trading base, possibly in order to facilitate trade between the two regions. (The word Lemba has a double meaning: 'to maintain cleanliness' and 'to bring trade to the people'.) Over time, however, the Buba clan established a city in Yemen, which they called Senna, and which is now referred to as Senna 1. They eventually became known as the BaSenna (the people of Senna).

Later, Senna 1 was abandoned and a second migration took place, this time led by the House of Hamisi, which had taken over leadership of the BaSenna. The migrants crossed into Africa, where they then split up. One group settled in Ethiopia and the other travelled down the east coast as far as Kenya and Tanzania, where they built a second city – called Senna 2.

In time, a small group moved inland from the coastal region to what is present-day Malawi, and the descendents of these people – who still live there today – are known as the BaMwenye, meaning 'Lords of the land'. Another group, this time led by the house of Bakali, continued to journey south and eventually settled in Mozambique where they built Senna 3, while another settlement, originally led by Seremane, was established at Chiramba in Zimbabwe and it is these latter migrants who became known as the Ba-Lemba. Using Chiramba as a base, further communities were established in Venda, and around modern-day Louis Trichardt, Polokwane (Pietersburg) and Tzaneen.[25]

Truth is stranger than fiction

The most remarkable element of Dr Mathivha's equally remarkable story is that it appears to be true. Evidence in support of this migration has been provided by Dr Tudor Parfitt, Director of the Centre for Jewish Studies at the School of Oriental and African Studies in London, whose interest in the Lemba was sparked a decade ago when he was invited to

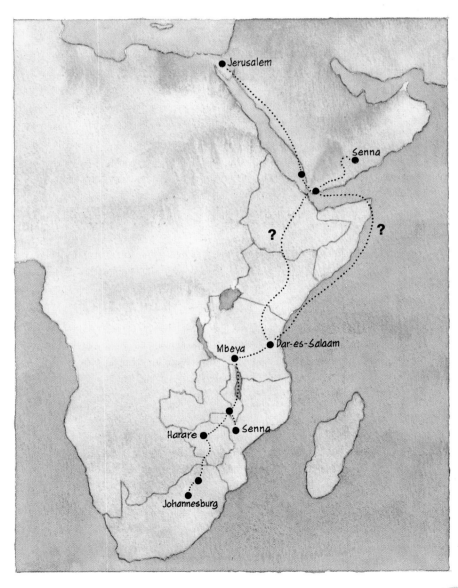

Below Historians studying the migration patterns of the Lemba have since established the possible route they may have taken as they moved south from the Middle East.

South Africa to give a lecture on Ethiopian Jews. His audience comprised mainly white South African Jews, but he noticed at the back of the hall a group of black people wearing *yarmulkes*, the Jewish skullcap. Once the lecture was over, Parfitt approached these unexpected visitors and, during their conversation, they described themselves as Jews from the Middle East. This is how he first learned of the Lemba.

Despite a degree of scepticism, Parfitt accepted an invitation to visit Venda for the weekend in order to meet the Lemba elders and learn more about the community and its ways. In fact, it was during this visit that he came to the conclusion that, despite the fact that the Lemba, like most other African communities, have had their oral history contaminated by Western influences, the origins of many of their traditions were clearly Semitic rather than African. But whether these traditions came from Islamic or Jewish sources was impossible to determine.

What Parfitt found particularly interesting was the fact that, unlike other tribes, the Lemba refused to intermarry and that they had a disdain for all other people, whom they referred to as *wasenzhi*, the gentiles. They also placed extraordinary importance on the ritual slaughter of animals, which is a practice most commonly associated with the Middle East.

As regards their origins, he was told, some-what enigmatically, that 'we came from the north, from a place called Senna. We left Senna, we crossed Pusela, we came to Africa and there we rebuilt Senna'.

Following in their footsteps

Armed only with this scanty evidence, Parfitt set out to prove the veracity – or otherwise – of the Lemba claims and, after 10 years of exhaustive research, he has been able to trace the migration of the Lemba from Yemen to South Africa with some accuracy, documenting his findings in his book, *Journey to the Vanished City*.

In an interview published in the *New York Times* in 1999[26], Parfitt described a visit he made to the Hadramawat region of Yemen, the site of former Jewish communities in the region. According to Dr Parfitt, when he mentioned the story of the migration of the Lemba to a religious leader of the holy city of Tarim, he was directed to a nearby village known as Senna.

'So I went off to find Senna,' he said. 'It's very remote and had never been visited by anyone before. The local tradition is that centuries ago the valley had been very fertile, irrigated by a dam, the ruins of which are still there. And then the dam burst, they think about a thousand years ago, and the people fled.'

A valley called the Wadi al-Masilah leads from Senna to a port on the Yemeni coast called Sayhut, which is about nine days' sailing from the coast of Africa, and Parfitt believes that the 'Pusela' of which the Lemba speak may be derived from Masila.

Further evidence in support of the Lemba migration is the fact that the Lemba have clan names like Sadiqui and Hamisi, which are 'clearly Semitic' and are also found in eastern Hadramawat.

So says the Old Testament

According to Dr Rudo Mathivha, an authority on Lemba history and traditions, the Lemba – like the Jews – believe there is only one god, whom they call Nwali and who is the creator of all things. On the holy day of the week, the Lemba praise Nwali and thank him for looking after them. Children are also taught to honour their mother and father.

Male children are circumcised at the age of eight. Although this relatively simple procedure is today, more often than not, carried out in hospitals, there is a growing feeling within the community that the ancient practice should once again be carried out by village elders in the home.

The Lemba do not eat pork, fish without scales, or any creature prohibited by the Old Testament and, like the Jewish faithful, their animals are ritually slaughtered by designated people and then bled. Just as kosher tradition dictates, they do not mix milk and meat in meal planning, and wash their hands before handling food or cooking utensils. The Lemba, too, have special burial rituals: graves are dug with a shelf for the body and the head always faces north, from where they are said to originate.

Lembas are encouraged to marry other Lembas, while a non-Lemba woman is instructed in Lemba ways – traditions, rituals and religious laws – and she is required to raise her children according to Lemba tradition. In fact, all Lemba children are taught from an early age that, according to oral tradition, the ancestors of the community migrated to southern Africa from the Middle East centuries, if not millennia, before.

Mathivha maintains that the Lemba would like to re-establish their links with the global Jewish community, to speak Hebrew and to learn about the Torah.

The genetic trail

This conclusion – that the Lemba are of Semitic origin – is also supported by research carried out by renowned South African geneticist Dr Himla Soodyall, head of the Medical Research Council's Human Genomic Diversity and Disease Research Unit, based at the University of the Witwatersrand.

'We can trace the genetic history of males through the Y chromosone, but we women don't have that,' Dr Soodyall explains. 'The mitochondrion DNA is passed down through the mother from daughter to daughter, and, using both these methods, we can trace the history of an individual.'[27]

According to Dr Himla Soodyall, her colleagues Dr Amanda Spurdle and Professor Trefor Jenkins were the first to describe the non-African contribution in the Lemba and that this work was further developed by a group of scientists led by Dr David Goldstein at the University of Oxford in the United Kingdom. David Goldstein's group was able to refine newer and more informative Y-chromosome markers, and were also responsible for describing the CMH.

'[The Lemba] have a strong oral history of non-African origins, and a culture similar to that practised by Semitic people, distinguishing them from other Bantu-speaking communities among whom they live,' adds Dr Soodyall. 'Their star sign is the Star of David with an elephant inside it. They have adopted the most stringent food laws based on Jewish custom: they don't eat meat or pork, or mix meat and milk products.

'What could have happened was that a dispute had arisen about succession in the Middle East, and the Arab ships did not come back to take these people. As they realised they were not going home, they began to marry with the local population, but they still kept their marriages within a small group.'

Dr Soodyall does, however, caution about being too dogmatic: 'At the moment, it is not possible to distinguish between Jewish and Arabic populations using current Y-chromosome markers, so making claims about "Jewish" or "Arabic" contributions in the Lemba may be premature. Also, we have no data from other populations along East Africa to confirm a "genetic trail". What this means is that we cannot confirm whether the CMH was present in the original male founding population of the Lemba, or whether it was introduced from another source more recently.'[28]

Dr Soodyall suggests that it is currently more accurate to use the term 'Middle Eastern' rather than 'Jewish' to describe the genetic signature of the Lemba.[29]

Remembering Zion

According to the 1996 census, approximately 75% of South Africa's population of about 43 million are practising Christians in one form or another and, of the various Christian churches, the Zion Christian Church (ZCC) is able to claim the largest affiliation. The ZCC has a congregation of over 4 million (9,71%), followed by the Nederduitse Gereformeerde Kerk (NGK) with about 3,8 million (8,85%) adherents. The Catholic church is supported by approximately 3,7 million (8,6%) and the Methodist church by 3.3 million (7,05%) worshippers. Pentecostal or charismatic churches account for a further 2,4 million (5,5%) of the population. In addition, there are about 600 000 Muslims and 580 000 Hindus in the country, while about 5 million (11,65%) South Africans have declared themselves as having 'no religion'.

The ZCC, which has about 4000 parishes throughout the country, was established in 1910 by Engenas Lekganyane in a rural area – later known as Zion City – in what is today the Limpopo Province. The congregation took its name in part from a similar community in Zion, Illinois, and in part from biblical references to Mount Zion, which in the Old Testament is the easternmost of the two hills of ancient Jerusalem, and the place where Yahweh, the God of Israel, dwells.

One of the distinguishing characteristics of the ZCC is that adherents believe in the healing power of faith. On occasion, this brings them into conflict with traditional African healers but, in general, the church respects traditional religious beliefs, especially those concerning the power of the ancestors to intercede with God on behalf of the living.

Zion City in Illinois, USA – which claims the motto 'Where God rules, man prospers' – was founded in 1900 by Dr John Alexander Dowie as 'a city of Christian ideal and in racial equality and intended to be a self-sufficient community'. Dowie's declared aim was 'to honour God and do good to all those within his reach'.*

In modern parlance, however, Zion and Zionism have a number of different connotations. Zion is often used in hymns and Christian literature to signify the heavenly city, or an earthly Utopia of brotherhood and love. It has also come to represent both the location of a Jewish homeland and the Zionist cause. Zionism, on the other hand, began in the 19th century and was a movement to establish a Jewish state in Palestine.

*From the article 'Zion, Illinois' written by William Schwager (www.ourzion.com)

Africa's astronaut: Mark Shuttleworth

Mark Shuttleworth was born in Welkom in the Free State on 18 September 1973. His parents later moved to Cape Town, where he attended Bishops High School and then the University of Cape Town, where he studied Business Science (Finance). It was in mid-1995, during his final year at university, that he founded Thawte Consulting, an Internet consulting business.

At first, Thawte operated out of Shuttleworth's parents' garage, his idea being to advise South African businesses on the use and applications of the Internet. The focus of the company soon shifted to Internet security, however, and in particular to the development of encryption and security systems related to electronic commerce. In 1996, having developed the first full-security e-commerce Web server commercially available outside the United States, Thawte became the first non-US based Certificate Authority. By 1999, the company had become the fastest-growing Internet Certificate Authority and the leading Certificate Authority outside of the United States.

What a bonus!

Towards the end of 1999, Shuttleworth had informed the staff at Thawte that negotiations were taking place with VeriSign, America's leading Certificate Authority, which had expressed an interest in buying the company. He had also made it clear that no one would lose his or her job or suffer financially if the deal went through. Needless to say, despite these reassurances, there was a lot of uncertainty among the staff.

It was only after Shuttleworth had clinched the deal with VeriSign that he called a meeting of all the staff to make the formal announcement, and informed his employees that they would each receive R1 million as their share of the company's good fortune.

'There was a room full of stunned faces,' Shuttleworth said. 'It was extraordinary. Some people were emotionally devastated... Other people were obviously thrilled to bits and excited on the telephone to friends and family.' [30]

As a VeriSign company, Thawte still remains autonomous in respect of its day-to-day business and, according to the Thawte Website, '...is still dedicated to increasing sales through good value for money, providing world-class customer service and growing our international penetration.'

Since the VeriSign deal, Shuttleworth has formed a new project team called HBD, which is short for 'Here Be Dragons', the phrase sometimes used to describe uncharted regions on early maps. HBD is a venture-capital company seeking to invest in innovative technology companies based in South Africa, but which have the potential to serve the global market. He has also endowed the Shuttleworth Foundation, a nonprofit organisation that supports educational innovation in Africa.

The age of space tourism is born...

In May 2001, American Dennis Tito paid $20 million for the privilege of flying from Baikonur Cosmodrome in Kazakhstan to the International Space Station (ISS), a geosynchronous orbit above the Earth, aboard a Soyuz space capsule. During his time in space, however, he spent most of his time enjoying the views from orbit and did not conduct any scientific studies. But whatever else Tito achieved, he had created a precedent and South Africa's Mark Shuttleworth was determined to follow in his footsteps. Like Tito, he began training in a Soyuz simulator while Space Adventures Ltd., a space tourism company, set about finalising a contract with the Russian Aviation and Space Agency.

Eventually, a deal was struck and Shuttleworth reputedly agreed to pay $20 million for a 10-day mission to the ISS in April 2002. With some of the preliminaries concluded, his intensive training programme began in earnest.

The 'world's first Afronaut'

Going on a space mission is not for the faint hearted. As part of his training, Shuttleworth had to undergo exhaustive medical examinations, participate in high-altitude supersonic jet flights and thoroughly familiarise himself with all aspects of the space capsule and details of the mission itself, especially since he intended to use the 10-day mission to carry out AIDS research. He also learnt to speak fluent Russian in the process.

'The training was frightening,' Shuttleworth told reporter Andrew Unsworth after his return to earth. 'I was scared and lonely, and I was getting a lot of flack from back home; people just didn't appreciate or understand what this could mean.

'So I sat there thinking, "Why am I doing this?" I wondered why I didn't get on a plane and get the hell out of there. But when you have a dream, there is no point in avoiding it; you've just got to keep going. Fortunately, the story ended well.'[31]

Above Since his trip to space, businessman, entrepreneur and one of South Africa's youngest self-made millionaires, Mark Shuttleworth has launched a successful nationwide campaign, furthering the development of mathematics and science in the national education system.

Eventually, after a gruelling eight months in Russia, Shuttleworth and his co-cosmonauts, Russian Yuri Gidzenko and Italian Roberto Vittori, blasted off from Baikonur Cosmodrome on 15 April 2002.

The take-off, says Shuttleworth, is 'very fast', and dark – at least to start with. This is because the windows of the Soyuz capsule in which the three astronauts ride are covered by fairings, which are only blown off as the space craft leaves the atmosphere. That is the first time the crew are able to get a glimpse of the Earth far below.

Two days later, the Soyuz space craft docked on the ISS and the three astronauts were able to transfer to the much larger orbiting space station. But the remaining eight days would be far from a holiday for the cosmonauts; there would be few comforts and no luxuries, and even sleeping was a problem...

'With no gravity or air convection, you breathe all the surrounding oxygen and replace it with carbon dioxide, which forms a bubble around your face. In the [sleeping] modules where we were first asked to sleep, they don't have much in the way of ventilation so we really struggled and found it very difficult to sleep. We then went to sleep in different spots on the station. You can sleep anywhere, strap yourself to the roof, hand on the wall, there is no up or down. You can fall asleep floating, but you will be pushed towards the air filters and they bump you awake.

'There is tons of stuff in the station and you have to stick everything down, put it behind a strap or tie it down. The things will even float out of your pockets, and it's incredibly difficult to find something in a bag because it's all floating and could just float out when you open it.

'In space, you become incredibly aware of what you've got in your hands because you need them when you move and to avoid bumping into things. There's lots of exposed metal, valves, pipes, wires and I've got the scars to prove it! You're not on a *Star Wars* aircraft; it's more like flying under the bonnet of a car.'[32]

The level of noise aboard the typical spacecraft would also amaze most people. Films like *Star Wars* and *Star Trek* give the completely mistaken impression that space travel is quiet and peaceful, where in reality the opposite is true. The life-support and other machinery aboard conventional spacecraft tend to generate so much noise that normal conversation is almost impossible. Some experts have raised concerns about the long-term effect of this constant deafening clatter on the hearing of astronauts, and it has been suggested that the most common word used on space flights is 'What?'

Return to Earth

On 5 May 2002, the three astronauts re-entered the Soyuz spacecraft and undocked from ISS for their return to Earth. This 400-kilometre journey involves re-entering the Earth's atmosphere at thousands of kilometres per hour, and then finally, making a parachute-assisted landing on the Russian steppes. With the heat shield disintegrating and a smell of burning inside the capsule, it was, says Mark Shuttleworth, 'a couple of minutes of being in heaven and hell at the same time.'

Back on terra firma, however, Mark Shuttleworth was fêted for his achievement around the world, not least of all in South Africa. At a special reception in his honour held in Pretoria on 3 June, President Thabo Mbeki thanked Shuttleworth for all he had done for South Africa and the African continent: 'He has shown us that the stars are accessible to us. We are grateful that he had the courage and vision to do what he did.'

What is a Certificate Authority?

Unencoded data transmitted between Web browsers and Websites is relatively easily intercepted by a third party and although this should not cause any serious problems – the Internet is a public communication network intended to facilitate a restriction-free exchange of information – an increasing amount of Web traffic is now private or confidential. An on-line purchaser, for example, needs to be assured that the credit-card information he or she supplies to an Internet vendor does not become freely available and is not able to be accessed by a fraudster. In other words, when someone visits a Website to make an on-line purchase, they need to know that the personal information they supply remains confidential. To achieve this, and in order to prevent any hackers from obtaining sensitive data, it is essential that certain messages be encrypted during transmission.

The most common method of encrypting data is called the SSL (Secure Sockets Layer) protocol. In simple terms, the Web browser 'interrogates' the Website before allowing a data exchange to take place. On being asked to present its 'bona fides', the Website presents a digital certificate to the Web browser. The browser then checks that a recognised Certificate Authority has issued the digital certificate in question – meaning there will be a safe and secure exchange of information – and the transaction is allowed to proceed. Thus, when you order a book from Kalahari.net or groceries from your local store via the Web, your Web browser – particularly if you're using Netscape Navigator or Internet Explorer – will confirm that the certificate presented by the site you are visiting has been issued by one of these authorities. You will almost certainly be unaware that this has happened, unless the site in question presents a certificate that is not recognised by your browser. When this happens, you will be alerted to the situation and given the option of confirming that you accept the certificate in question – in other words, you will have to decide between continuing with the transaction at your own risk, or terminating the contact.

SSL Server Certificates allow buyers and sellers to communicate securely. It effectively protects both parties; it means that the seller can accept credit-card information with confidence and, at the same time, protects the buyer's sensitive personal information. It also ensures that hackers are not able to read your e-mail messages. In exchange for this service, Website owners pay a fee to the Certificate Authority. This fee is currently in the region of $125 per annum.

In December 1999, the Netcraft Secure Server Survey attributed 41 per cent of the global SSL certificate market to Thawte. In the same month, VeriSign, the leading Certificate Authority, acquired Thawte for $575 million – that is, over R5 billion!

In response, Shuttleworth said he was filled with pride walking to the rocket with a badge of the South African flag on his spacesuit.

'There is so much to be proud of in South Africa today. On my way here, we stopped at a red traffic light, and a young entrepreneur stepped up to the car and placed a small globe on the bonnet. He made me realise two things. One was that entrepreneurship is alive and well in South Africa as he tried to sell me two globes. The other was that the globe seemed to be upside down, with the south pole on top. Then I thought to myself: there is, in fact, no sign in space saying north should be on top. I think that it is time that the southern hemisphere should be on top.'[33]

Manned exploration of space

The first spacecraft, the Soviet Union's *Sputnik 1*, was launched on 4 October 1957, but many more unmanned spacecraft, launched both by the Soviet Union and the United States, would follow in the years that were to come. The first manned space flight occurred on 12 April 1961, when the Soviet spacecraft *Vostok 1* carried Russian cosmonaut Yuri Gagarin into orbit.

Three weeks later, American astronaut Alan B Shepard Jnr rode a Mercury space capsule named *Freedom 7* on a 15-minute, 486-kilometre sub-orbital flight, and the following month American President John F Kennedy committed the United States to landing a manned spacecraft on the moon 'before the decade is out'. The name given to this programme was Apollo, after the sun god from Greek mythology. Nine months later, on 20 February 1962, in one of the final missions in the Mercury programme, John H Glenn, flying in a *Freedom 7* capsule powered by an Atlas rocket, made the first manned orbital flight carried out by the United States.

There were no fewer than 17 missions in the Apollo Programme. *Apollo 11*, carrying the now world-famous team of astronauts Neil A Armstrong, Edwin (Buzz) Aldrin and Michael Collins blasted off from Cape Canaveral on 16 July 1969, with Armstrong and Aldrin landing on the moon four days later. (Collins remained in space, orbiting the moon in the lunar orbiting module.) *Apollo 17* was the last mission to carry astronauts to the moon in December 1972.

Unlike the United States, the Soviet Union concentrated on unmanned – that is, robotic – exploration of the moon, and no Russian cosmonaut has thus set foot on the lunar surface. Nevertheless, the Russian Soyuz spacecraft were the first to be launched in 1967, the upgraded Soyuz T series being introduced only after 1980. In the years that followed, these Russian spacecraft were regularly used to ferry cosmonauts and supplies to orbiting space stations.

Generally speaking, spacecraft – as opposed to launch vehicles – are essentially non-powered and use initial momentum coupled with gravitational forces to travel through space. Manoeuvring is achieved through the use of small onboard liquid-fuel rocket engines. The main exception was the Apollo programme's lunar landing craft. This craft was powered by a rocket capable of lifting it off the surface of the moon and returning it to the orbiting *Apollo* craft, which in turn had sufficient rocket power to pull itself out of lunar orbit for the return journey to Earth.

Spacecraft are extremely complex machines that are made up of literally millions of components and have to be constructed to be 99 9999 per cent reliable. If the average motor car was built to the same tolerances, it would run for about 100 years before experiencing its first malfunction.

Did you know?

It took South African Mark Shuttleworth only four years to earn R5 billion.

The ostrich-foot people

Deep in the Zambezi valley lies a remote community called the Vadoma that is affected by a rare medical condition called ectrodactyly. This genetic condition – the word comes from the Greek *ektroma*, which means 'abortion' and *daktylos*, which means 'finger' – causes a malformation of the hands and feet, and is characterised by the absence of one or more fingers or toes. Those afflicted by this condition are variously described as the ostrich-footed people, the goat-footed people, the cloven-hoofed people, The-Ones-Who-Hide-Behind-Their-Fingers, and even as the Touvingas ('two-fingers').

According to some stories, the ostrich-foot people are said to be 'bewitched' or possessed of miraculous powers, and are said to be able to run like the wind and climb trees with the speed and agility of monkeys. The truth, unfortunately, is more prosaic.

Ectrodactyly: The medical condition

It has now been established that ectrodactyly is part of a bigger syndrome, called the EEC syndrome, which comprises (E) ectrocadtyly, (E) ectodermal dysplasia (a malformation of the skin) and (C) cleft palate. This condition has been recorded in medical journals for hundreds of years, and in 1964 the American edition of the *Journal of Joint and Bone Surgery* included the following account:

Top right A cave painting at Maclear in the Eastern Cape indicates the presence of similarly limbed individuals in the area in years gone by.
Below A number of the forms depicted on the Maclear cave walls have been interpreted as representative of ectrodactyly.

'The earliest reference to congenial hand deformities of any type generally occurred in works dealing with so-called monsters. These accounts were so clouded in hearsay, myth and superstition that it is hard to identify the anomaly. Even in the 18th and 19th centuries, when there was a more scientific approach, the descriptions were ambiguous and drawings were by no means clear.'[34]

According to the same journal, the renowned French physician, Ambriose Paré (1510–90), who is regarded by some as the father of modern surgery, made the first reference in this medical condition in the late 16th century.

'In the year 1573,' Paré wrote, 'I saw in Paris, at the Porte de St André-des-Arts, a child of nine years of age, born in Parpeuille, a village three leagues from Guise; his father was called Pierre Renard, and his mother who bore him, Marquette Renard. This monster had only two fingers on his right hand and his arm was quite well formed from the shoulder to the elbow, but was greatly deformed from the elbow to the two fingers.'[35]

This, however, was not a case of ectrodactly, but hemimolia (or longitudinal limb deficiency), which occurs when an embryo fails to properly develop during pregnancy, and the first time a link was drawn between ectrodactyly – cleft hands and feet – and cleft lip and cleft palate occurred in 1804 and is attributed to Dr Franz Heinrich Martens.

 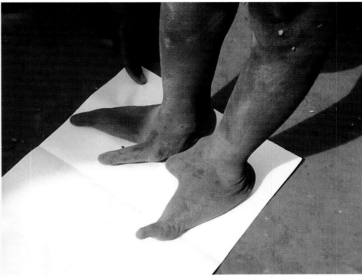

Malady of the modern day

In 1971, Professor Gelfand from the University of Rhodesia described the case of Mabarani Nyakutepa, a member of the Vadoma tribe from Kanyemba in Zimbabwe. In his report, he wrote: 'X-rays of both feet were similar and confirmed the presence of bidactyly – namely, a large and little toe with the entire absence of the second, third and fourth toes... An interesting finding was a slight [but] definite webbing between the third and fourth fingers (between the middle and the ring finger) of the right hand, the skin here extending two-thirds of an inch beyond the proximal interphalangeal joint. There was no such change in the left hand. The rest of the physical examination revealed nothing of interest; and Mabarani, who was five feet, five inches tall appeared otherwise normal; the deformity was a slight handicap in movement, and running in particular was difficult.'[36]

In 1984 Professors Beighton and Viljoen from the University of Cape Town Medical School also made a study of the Talaunda tribe from Botswana, who were similarly affected by the condition. The following is an extract from their report:

'Their age ranged from 8 [months] to 50 [years], and their hands and feet were involved in every instance. Pre-axial polydactyly and triphalangeal thumbs, absent digits and soft tissue and bony syndactyly were present, but no individual had the true "lobster claw" abnormality of the hands. In every instance, the hand abnormalities were less severe than those of the feet.

'The foot anomaly was severe in all five affected persons examined. The central metatarsal rays were absent and there was variable fusion of the first, second, fourth and fifth metatarsophalgeal structures. These digits were curved towards the central cleft, with additional deviation of the phalanges. The malformed feet often resulted in pain after prolonged standing and, although balance was remarkably well preserved, walking was stilted and ungainly.'[37]

The curiosities of the Vadoma

In recent times, South African researcher Johan le Roux has also made an exhaustive study of the Vadoma. According to his unpublished thesis, *Vimbai: The Story of the Ostrich-footed People*, the Vadoma arrived in Zimbabwe about 250 years ago, and then split into two groups, one group settling in the Chewore and Kanyemba area and the other in Angwa.

Top left and above The unusually high incidence of the rare genetic condition ectrodactyly in the hands and feet of the Vadoma people of the Zambezi valley has led to them being known in some circles as the 'ostrich-foot people'.

Below Especially when it is compared to that of a human (top), the foot of an ectrodactyly sufferer bears only a passing resemblance to that of both the gorilla (centre) and the chimpanzee (bottom).

According to oral tradition, the original chief of the Angwa group was a woman, who ordered that her people remain within the valley. They were not to leave to find work, nor were they to marry outside of the clan. 'It was this injunction', Le Roux speculates, 'that severely restricted the size of the gene pool within the community, and eventually led to the development of ectrodactyly.'[38]

Biologist Dr Stephen Lewis of Liverpool University's Chester College supports this view. In a paper titled 'Not Just Making Babies – A Darwinian Perspective', which was delivered in 2001, Lewis declared:

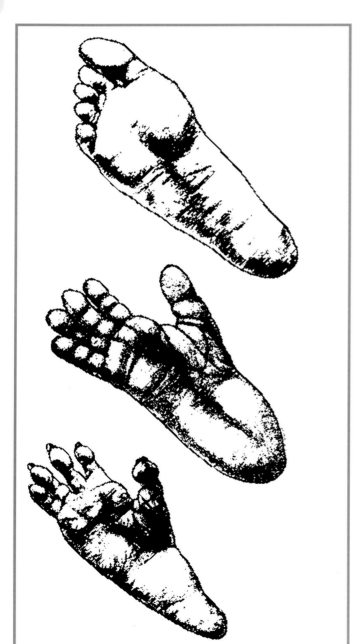

'[Ectrodactyly] is inherited as an autosomal dominant condition with variable penetrance. The gene that produces it is on the long arm of chromosome number seven. While affecting the hands, it can also affect the feet. Thus, in Africa there is what are called "ostrich-footed" people. In particular, there are two tribes, the Wadomo of the Zambezi valley in Zimbabwe and the Kalanga of the eastern Kalahari in Botswana. The condition is not confined to Africa, though. Until recently, there was a well-documented family with affected hands and feet that formed part of a famous American travelling freak show and probably the best slide guitarist I've ever heard – playing in a street band I happened upon in San Francisco 17 years ago – clearly had ectrodactyly displayed in both his hands. So it is not necessarily a condition that mitigates against useful life.

'There is a story relating how the gene became established in Africa. I can't vouch for its total accuracy but I did hear it in academic circles. It states that there was a tribe in which a child with ectrodactyly was born and that this was greeted with great concern that evil spirits had been at work and that the child could not be allowed to remain with the tribe. In such cultures, abnormal births are sometimes viewed as being essentially non-human. Some have it that it is not a deformed human child that has been born but really a hippopotamus and, that being the case, it should be placed with its own kind – in the river. And so it left the tribe. The story goes that a second child with ectrodactyly was born (presumably to the same family) and that it went the way of the first. Then a third child with this condition was born. This time it was decided that it was the gods who were really at work and that they wanted this child to be left with its family. And so, over time the gene for ectrodactyly, having been allowed to remain, became established as a characteristic of that tribe.'[39]

There are other explanations put forward for this condition, however. For example, when Le Roux visited the Zambezi valley to interview and photograph the Vadoma, a local police chief informed him that they (the Vadoma) had the 'disgusting habit... where they chopped off the fingers and toes of little babies', but also expressed his sincere relief that this practice had now been discontinued.

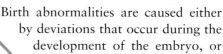
The stuff of myth and legend

Birth abnormalities are caused either by deviations that occur during the development of the embryo, or as a consequence of genetic mutation. In modern times, there have also been cases where malformed births have been the result of the ingestion of certain drugs. In the late 1950s and early 1960s, for example, an alarming number of deformed babies were born to women who had taken the sedative, thalidomide, during pregnancy.

In ancient times, the most extreme examples of these birth malformations were regarded as monsters because of their physical appearance. A birth of this nature was also seen to portent of evil and, in all likelihood, led to the creation of some if not all of the mythical 'monsters' that exist in folklore such as the Cyclops, sirens, mermaids and possibly even giants and dwarfs.

English physician William Harvey made the first objective investigation of malformations in the 17th century, but French anatomists Étienne and Isidore Geoffroy Saint-Hilaire undertook the first detailed scientific study of the phenomenon. Their *Traité de Teratologie* in 1836 laid the basis for the study of teratology – the study of malformation and abnormal growths.

Unfortunately, in latter-day South Africa, certain extreme right-wing groups use the spurious fact that some black people have 'animal feet' as 'proof' that blacks are more animal-like than whites. It is important to remember, however, that ectrodactyly is not a condition that affects black people only. It affects people of all colours and creeds and has been observed in many parts of the world. In fact, cases of ectrodactyly and its related condition syndactyly – where digits are fused to create what is commonly referred to a 'web-footing' – have been reported not only in Europe, North and South America and Africa, but also among other primates. There are well-documented cases where this affliction has been observed in marmoset monkeys and gorillas, for example.

Although ectrodactyly appears to be variable, in that it manifests itself in a number of ways and may skip generations, it seems that affected males often produce an excess of affected sons. Studies suggest that this condition affects about 1 in 90 000 of the population.

Top left The ectrodactyly foot is not at all similar to that of a primate (see opposite). There is no mobile opposable 'thumb' and the foot structure means that balance is very difficult.

An interesting footnote...

Johan le Roux suggests that the first recorded evidence of ectrodactyly in southern Africa may be found in a rock painting at Maclear in the Eastern Cape. Two of the individuals in this painting clearly appear to exhibit deformities usually associated with ectrodactyly. This theory is, however, disputed by some academics who argue that since most rock paintings were made while the painter was in a trance-like state, they are not meant to be seen as depictions of the 'real' world, but merely as representations of the images that existed in the mind of their creator. In other words, the two figures Le Roux has identified as possibly representing individuals who are suffering from ectrodactyly may merely be drawings of spirits, demons or imagined creatures that existed only in the mind of the painter. In the final analysis, however, you be the judge...

Endnotes

1. Interview with the author.
2. Ibid.
3. *National Geographic*, 14 August 1997.
4. David Derbyshire, 'Human family meets its oldest ancestor', *Sunday Times*, 14 July 2002 (first published in *The Telegraph*, London).
5   Ibid.
6. Chris Barron, 'So Many Questions' (Interview with Professor Phillip Tobias), *Sunday Times*, 21 July 2002.
7. J B Peires, *The House of Phalo* (1987), Johannesburg: Ravan Press, p. 108.
8. Ibid., p. 209
9. 'Evidence of R Daniels', *Minutes of the Proceedings of the Court of Inquiry... on the fate of the Caffir Chief Hintsa* (Cape Town, 1837), in J B Peires, op. cit.
10. Monday Paper, Volume 16 Number 12, 12–19 May 1997, Department of Development and Public Affairs, Cape Town: University of Cape Town.
11. Gail Smith, 'Why we froth about Saartjie', *The Star*, 22 May 2002.
12. Pippa Skotnes (ed.), *Miscast – Negotiating the Presence of the Bushmen* (1996), Cape Town: University of Cape Town, p. 70.
13. Ibid.
14. Ibid.
15. Ibid., p. 350.
16. A P Cartwright, *West Driefontein – Ordeal by Water*, West Driefontein Gold Mine, pp. 7–8.
17. Ibid., p. 80.
18. Ibid., p. 12/13.
19. Ibid., p. 80.
20. Ibid., p. 80.
21. Ibid., p. 10.
22. Ibid., p. 28.
23. Ibid.,. p. viii.
24. Figures provided by Goldfields, South Africa.
25. Dr Rudo Mathivha, Lecture: Zionist Lunch Club, Johannesburg, 15 October 1999.
26. Nicholas Wade, 'DNA back South Africa tribe's tradition of early descent from the Jews', *New York Times*, 9 May 1999.
27. 'Africa's history is in our genes', *The Star*, 11 July 2002.
28. Personal e-mail message to the author.
29. The author gratefully acknowledges the kind assistance of Terence Stirling, Thalia Anderson and Dr Himla Soodyall in the compilation of this segment.
30. Interview with Mark Shuttleworth, www.africaninspace.com/home/mission/faq/leadership
31. Andrew Unsworth, 'Seeing stars where others see limits' (interview with Mark Shuttleworth), *Sunday Times*, 2 June 2002.
32. Ibid.
33. Corlene Barrett, 'Mark and Mbeki do the astro jive', *The Star*, 3 June 2002.
34. Johan le Roux, *Vimbai – The Story of the Ostrich-footed People* (unpublished thesis), p. 38.
35. Ibid.
36. Ibid.
37. P Beighton and D L Viljoen (1984), 'The Split-Hand and Split-Foot Anomaly in a Central African Negro Population', *American Journal of Medical Genetics*, Volume 19, pp. 545–52.
38. Johan le Roux (unpublished thesis), op. cit., p. 28.
39. Dr Stephen Lewis, 'Not Just Making Babies – A Darwinian Perspective' (paper presented at the 'New Genetics: Critical Perspectives' Conference), University of Liverpool: Chester College, www.chester.ac.uk/-sjlewis/DM/Babies

Index

*Note: Page references in **bold** denote illustrated content.*